Five Life Stages

of

NONPROFIT ORGANIZATIONS

JUDITH SHARKEN SIMON

WITH

J. TERENCE DONOVAN

FIELDSTONE
ALLIANCE

SAINT PAUL
MINNESOTA

We thank The David and Lucile Packard Foundation and
the Amherst H. Wilder Foundation for support of this publication.

Fieldstone Alliance
An imprint of Turner Publishing Company

445 Park Avenue, 9th Floor
New York, NY 10022
Phone: (646)291-8961   Fax: (646)291-8962

200 4th Avenue North, Suite 950
Nashville, TN 37219
Phone: (615)255-2665   Fax: (615)255-5081

www.turnerpublishing.com
www.fieldstonealliance.com

Fieldstone Alliance is committed to strengthening the performance of the nonprofit sector. Through the synergy of its consulting, training, publishing, and research and demonstration projects, Fieldstone Alliance provides solutions to issues facing nonprofits, funders, and the communities they serve. Fieldstone Alliance was formerly Wilder Publishing and Wilder Consulting departments of the Amherst H. Wilder Foundation. If you would like more information about Fieldstone Alliance and our services, please contact

Fieldstone Alliance
60 Plato Boulevard East, Suite 150
Saint Paul, MN 55107

800-274-6024
www.FieldstoneAlliance.org

Edited by Vincent Hyman
Designed and illustrated by Rebecca Andrews
Cover designed by Kirsten Nielsen

Manufactured in the United States of America
Fourth printing, March 2010

Library of Congress Cataloging-in-Publication Data

Sharken Simon, Judith, 1962-
    The five life stages of nonprofit organizations : where you are, where you're going, and what to expect when you get there / by Judith Sharken Simon with J. Terence Donovan.
        p. cm.
    Includes bibliographical references.
    ISBN 13: 978-0-940069-22-0 (pbk.)
    ISBN 10: 0-940069-22-9 (pbk.)
    1. Nonprofit organizations--United States--Management.
    2. Nonprofit organizations--United States--Management--Evaluation. 3. Organizational change--United States. 4. Strategic planning--United States. I. Donovan, J. Terence, 1951- II. Title.
    HD62.6 .S49 2001
    658'.048--dc21

                    2001026343

This book is dedicated to Vijit Ramchandani.
My colleague and friend who, in life as in his passing,
understood and taught the intricate dynamics of life.

Contents

About the Authors

JUDITH SHARKEN SIMON is an organization consultant who has worked with nonprofits for over fifteen years. She has led numerous data-gathering efforts involving focus groups, interviews, and surveys. In her consulting role, Judy assists clients with nonprofit organization development, including life stage transitions, strategic planning, and board development. Judy has a master's degree in organization development from the University of Minnesota and is the author of *The Fieldstone Alliance Nonprofit Field Guide to Conducting Successful Focus Groups* (1999). Judy has worked extensively with the Saint Paul and Minneapolis area Southeast Asian communities. She developed and coordinated the Southeast Asian Leadership Program and has served as a consultant, supervisor, and instructor for the Bicultural Training Partnership. Judy has also been a senior consultant with Community Services Group of the Amherst H. Wilder Foundation, a project manager for a county government human services department, a mentorship coordinator in human resource development, and a public workshop trainer on focus groups and other topics related to nonprofit management. In her work, she has consulted with small, grassroots organizations and large government entities—new and old.

J. TERENCE DONOVAN holds a B.A. in economics from Middlebury College and an M.S. in management from Saint Mary's College. He has done postgraduate work in criminal justice at Southern Illinois University. He is an independent consultant and a partner with consultant Janet Hagberg of Personal Power Products. Personal Power Products develops and distributes standardized assessment instruments that measure individual learning styles and stages of personal power in organizations. He has been developing standardized instruments for twenty years. His experience includes strategic planning, organization development, management coaching, planning, grant management, evaluation, and contract management.

Preface

Nonprofit organizations are the binding threads of the United States' social fabric. More than one million such organizations exist. They employ more than ten million people, serve untold numbers of people, and fill in service gaps left by the public and private sectors. Nonprofit organizations are becoming important players in other countries as well.

Despite the number and importance of nonprofit organizations, little has been documented about their growth and development—at least when compared to the business sector. Yet, after more than a decade of consulting with nonprofit organizations, I have become acutely aware of how important such information is. Without a framework for thinking about the developmental stages of their nonprofit organization, those engaged with them are vulnerable to unnecessary struggles. As an organization development consultant my role is to assess an organization's situation and design and implement interventions which will help it grow. An understanding of the organization's stage of life helps.

The concept of "organization life stages" is intuitive. Those of us who work for or consult with nonprofit organizations or businesses (or both) quickly size up an organization as being in some stage of "start-up," "maturity," or "demise." There is ample published literature in the business sector that confirms our instincts, but less is available pertaining to nonprofit organizations; however, there have been some. Of particular note are the articles and presentations on nonprofit life cycles by Sue Stevens of the Stevens Group at LarsonAllen, Paul Connolly of the Conservation Company, Karl Mathiasen III of the Nonprofit Center for Nonprofit Boards, and Carter McNamara of the Management Assistance Program for Nonprofits. Other work in this area is mentioned in the Appendix. What I hope to do in this book is put forward one version of the stages of nonprofit organization development that it is widely accessible to the large numbers of people connected to the nonprofit sector. Over time, results from the use of the assessment tool included with this work may help us gain a better understanding of the validity of this model and improve our use of it when helping organizations develop.

Judith Sharken Simon
May 2001

Acknowledgments

The development of the model I present here has been an interest and passion of mine for a very long time. Since I started my career, I have been intrigued by the psychology of organizational life and its impact on the people who work within organizational systems. I am indebted to Amherst H. Wilder Foundation for providing the flexibility, encouragement, standards of excellence, and principle of professional development I have enjoyed during my tenure. Truly, my colleagues are my role models, my cheerleaders, and the people with whom I feel most privileged to work.

I am grateful to the many clients I have worked with over the years who provided excellent material to help me develop and support the model. They, and the many reviewers, also deserve thanks for the insightful critique and unwavering support of its creation.

A special thanks to those people who reviewed the field test draft of this book:

I offer special thanks to Pat Peterson, Terry Donovan, Dave Sharken, Emil Angelica,

Judy Alnes	Dawn Fisk Thomsen	Elaine Lilly
Richard Alvarado	Rose Mary Fry	Sandra Lovett
Beth Applegate	Nina Gregg	Carol Lukas
Nancy Axelrod	Joyce Gregor	Paul Mattessich
Janet Ballew Patterson	Mary Anne Guillot	Hans Neuhauser
Bryan Barry	William Hall	Judith Pfeffer
Mary H. Beck	Beth Harper Briglia	Jeanine M. Prickett
Sharon Behar	Mimi Hoffman	Mary Sabatke
Bill Belcher	Ginger Hope	Elizabeth Sadlon
Sue Bennett	Alan Hough	Roselma Samala
Jacqueline Bentz	Barb Jeanetta	Anita Sanborn
Mark I. Berger	Lisa R. Johnson	Elizabeth Schaffer
Jane Bowers	Tom Kingston	David Sharken
Paula Buchanan	Holly Korda	Karen Simmons
Mike Burns	Carolyn Kourofsky	Paul Sturm
Paul Connolly	Mari Lane Gewecke	Jim Vaillancourt
Cindy Coy	Theo. R. Leverenz	Diane Vinokur-Kaplan
Marjorie Davis	Henry D. Lewis	Judy Wagner
Marilyn L. Donnellan	Lynda Lieberman Baker	Joan Wells

and Patti Tototzintle who encouraged me to publish on this topic. I also thank Gary Leske of the University of Minnesota, who was a steadfast advisor in my initial pursuit of the topic during my graduate studies, and Vince Hyman whose editorial skill and style are treasured gifts. Thanks as well to Joan Wells of Resources and Counseling for the Arts for the fascinating case study she contributed to this book and to Marjorie Davis for her insights on the role of volunteers in organization development.

Finally, I want to acknowledge my family: my parents and siblings, whose lives have helped shape mine; and my daughters, Tahlia and Maya, who should be commended for putting up with all those hours when Mommy wasn't available. And of course, my husband, Chris, who provided childcare while I researched and wrote, lent his math and logic expertise to the development of the assessment tool, and provided endless hours of emotional fortitude.

Introduction

OPERA STAR LEONTYNE PRICE once said, "Know when you're shifting gears in life. You should leave your era; it should never leave you."[1] Shifting gears *is* a part of life, for people as well as organizations. Knowing when and how to shift gears—as well as what each gear feels like—is what this book is about. Reading it will help people in the nonprofit sector feel less isolated, know what's normal, plan for the future, put problems in context, and manage transitions more effectively.

You already know quite a bit about shifting gears. You've had to shift gears in your own maturation, from infant to toddler, child, teen, young adult, and adult. If you've had experiences working with organizations of different sizes and ages, you've probably witnessed various changes, from mild to disastrous, brought on by transitions in leadership, industry, the economy, or other factors. Various books, most of them aimed at for-profit businesses, have documented life cycle changes in organizations. These tell us that

- Organizations evolve naturally.
- Organizational leaders have specific roles in each stage of development.
- Leadership changes are inevitable and necessary.
- Factors such as age of the organization, size of the organization, industry in which the organization is embedded, and societal interests trigger transitions.

Much of this is true for nonprofit organizations, as well, but their unique culture makes for variations on the theme. This book describes the life cycle stages of nonprofit organizations as experienced and described (to the author and in the literature)

---

[1] As quoted in Chambliss et al. (1991, 45).

by nonprofit leaders and the consultants who work with them. Armed with the knowledge of nonprofit life cycle stages, staff, management, boards, and funders can better serve their constituencies. Leaders and organizations that skillfully project future needs, make decisions proactively, and anticipate challenges are generally more successful. In addition, knowing that the stress staff and organizations are experiencing is normal and inevitable—not a sign of incompetence or impending disaster—will ease the burden of many nonprofit leaders. The ability of nonprofit leadership to recognize and address critical junctures in the life of the organization is vital to the success of the organization, and ultimately the nonprofit sector.

Who This Book Is For

This book was written to help nonprofit leaders and managers, board members, organization development consultants, and funders.

- *Leaders and managers.* Nonprofit leaders who understand the developmental stages of their organizations will be able to anticipate and prepare for organizational transitions.

- *Board members.* Nonprofit board members, who often come from the business sector, may have little knowledge of the culture of the nonprofit sector or the normal organizational progression of a nonprofit. Training on the life stages model will help board members fulfill their roles as stewards of the organization, wherever they hail from.

- *Organization development consultants.* Organization development consultants should be well versed in the model of how nonprofit organizations grow and develop. Since consultants are often hired when a nonprofit is in one of the life stage transitions, this model will assist them in helping the organization understand and address its issues. A guide to the model for consultants is included at the end of the book.

- *Funders.* Funders can use this book to assist them in drawing conclusions about the capacity of organizations they support or are considering supporting. For example, start-up organizations may require resources to develop administrative systems while more mature organizations with solid administrative systems already in place may require resources to rethink their strategic direction and re-ground themselves in their community.

How This Book Is Organized

This book has four sections.

This chapter presents the stages of nonprofit organization development, including a case study illustrating how an organization typically progresses through these stages and an explanation of the assumptions that underlie the life stages model. It includes a detailed description of each stage, highlighting typical organizational situations, opportunities, and obstacles likely to be encountered, and general advice about what organizations in each stage need to focus on in order to move successfully to the next life stage. Tips are offered to emphasize the overall concern and approach of each stage and to suggest key activities in the seven arenas of each stage: governance, staff leadership, financing, administrative systems, staffing, products and services, and marketing.

This tool can help organizations determine what life stage they are in and their organization's probable strengths and weaknesses relative to that stage.

This chapter contains case studies that illustrate factors to attend to in each life stage and strategies to address those factors.

This includes a consultant's guide to the life stages assessment tool, recommended reading, other useful resources, and notes on the development and testing of the assessment tool.

A Model Is Just a Model

This book outlines a typical path of development for an average nonprofit organization. No organization exactly mirrors the progression outlined in this book. Some move deftly through their life stages, others get stuck in one stage for significant periods of time. Every organization is unique, yet there are patterns and similarities across organizations. The model described in this book gives names to those patterns and should be used as a guide to refer to as the organization grows and develops.

There are certain types of organizations for which the model seems less helpful. These include the following:

- *Very large, complex organizations*

  While very large, complex organizations will certainly recognize the stages outlined in this book, they will find it difficult to place their entire organization in one stage. Leaders in such organizations may want to think of each division or department as a separate organization with its own life cycle. Further analysis of the extent to which different departments or divisions are in different stages could also yield helpful information to management.

- *Very small, grassroots organizations*

  Some organizations purposely remain small and informal. Because the model is based on an assumption of intentional growth and accompanying formal systems, it does not apply readily to such organizations. While these organizations may not identify with the particular stages, they may find value in analyzing their organization in light of the seven arenas described in chapter one and use the analysis to pinpoint strengths, weaknesses, opportunities, and threats to the organization's vitality.

- *Organizations with unique circumstances*

  Some organizations do not operate within the traditional framework found in the nonprofit sector. Such circumstances may include unique board structures; organizations serving or comprised of people from nonwestern cultures; reliance on nontraditional sources of funding; operating in a highly collaborative manner; subsidiaries of larger, more established organizations; or organizations with exponential growth. Organizations such as these will find this model is built on more commonly known and used nonprofit systems and structures. As with very small, grassroots organizations, organizations with particular, unique situations may use this book to analyze their organization in light of the seven arenas and use the analysis to identify challenges and opportunities.

Caveats aside, the majority of nonprofit organizations should recognize themselves in the patterns described in this book and be more successful as an organization because of the insights they gain regarding their life stage.

The next chapter will introduce you to some assumptions about nonprofit organizations, life stages, an image of the developmental path, and a detailed description of each of the stages of development.

Chapter One

Organizational Life Stages

T O HELP YOU NAVIGATE the model, several pieces of groundwork need to be laid: a brief *synopsis* of the model and the five stages, the underlying *premises* upon which the model rests, and the *seven arenas* used to describe the intricacies of organizational life in each stage. These three components should help you understand the overall model, to apply the assessment tool to your organization, and to make plans based on the stage your organization is in.

The Stages of Organizational Development

Nonprofit organizations typically move through five stages of development. To help you remember the stages, each has a short two-word title and accompanying graphic image. The titles and images are meant to be brief descriptors of the primary tone or activity for that stage. As you will see, an organization's life really is a journey of sorts, with many choices, challenges, and obstacles along the way. Let's explore briefly the five stages of organizational life.

Stage One: Imagine and Inspire

This is the vision or idea stage, where the organization is not yet formalized and where imagination and inspiration abound. The primary question at this stage is, "Can this dream be realized?" This stage is characterized by lots of enthusiasm, energy, and creativity, but at this point, the organization really is merely a dream of a better world that is inspirational and worth striving for.

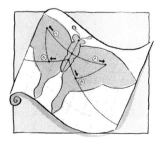

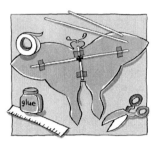

Stage Two: Found and Frame

This is the start-up phase of the organization, when it receives its official nonprofit status and all the activities of founding and framing an organization occur. The key question at this stage is "How are we going to pull this off?" Like Stage One, this stage is characterized by excitement and high levels of interest by many people, accompanied by the fear that formalizing the dream will result in the loss of its magic. The act of incorporating formally establishes the organization.

Stage Three: Ground and Grow

In this stage the organization is concerned with building its foundation by grounding its activities and growing the "business." The overriding question is "How can we build this to be viable?" Organizations in this stage are focused on establishing systems of accountability; however, the need for growth on multiple fronts may be overwhelming to those running the organization. The Ground and Grow stage has a mundane feel of "taking care of business"; but it also has numerous enticing intersections, choices, and challenges.

Stage Four: Produce and Sustain

This is the mature phase of the organization's life when production is at its peak and sustaining the organization is a high priority. The primary concern, "How can the momentum be sustained?" The organization is very stable, yet that same stability may make it stale as concerns for procedure slow creativity and growth. Stage Four is a productive place that, at its peak, feels a little like automatic pilot. Staff are doing their work effectively and enthusiastically.

Stage Five: Review and Renew

In this stage the organization is reinventing itself in some way, shape, or form through a process of review and renewal. The primary question is "What do we need to redesign?" It can be a time of large or small, exciting or stressful, but always necessary, change. Proponents of chaos theory will recognize that in order for organizations to be as viable as possible, they will need to operate in modes that promote chaos and therefore create possibilities for new patterns of interaction to form. Mature nonprofits revisit one or more aspects of their organization—mission, vision, products, services, structure—sometimes changing them drastically, sometimes only making slight innovations, as they rediscover who they are and how they fit in the changing world. Relative to the scope of the modifications, organizations may cycle back to an earlier stage. For example, if the change relates to the primary mission of the organization it may find itself back in Stage Two, while minor alterations in the organizational structure may simply mean revisiting Stage Four.

Decline and Dissolution

Sometimes it happens—an organization is forced or chooses to shut its doors. In this model, decline and dissolution is *not* considered an inevitable stage of an organization's life cycle but rather one of the routes an organization can find itself taking. That is why I describe only five stages. An organization can face dissolution at any stage. There are several indicators (see page 39) that signify an organization is seriously declining.

Figure 1, The Model of Nonprofit Organization Life Stages, illustrates the nonprofit organization's developmental path.

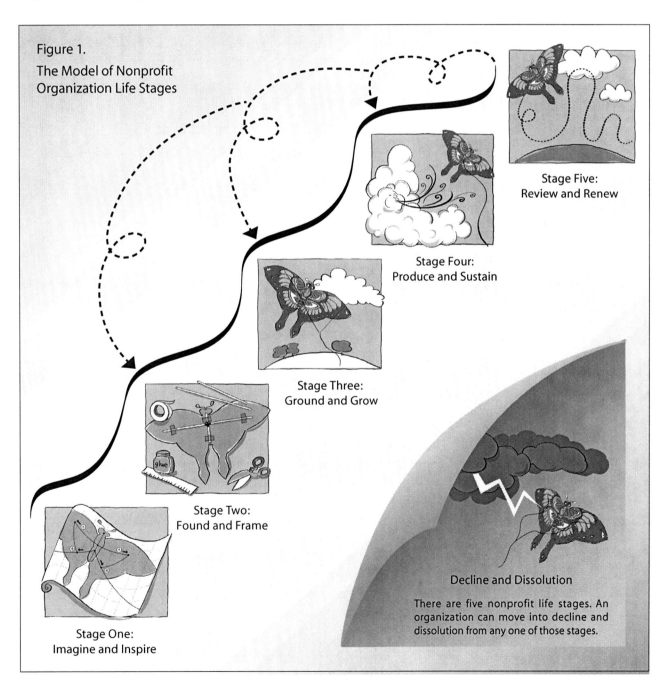

Figure 1.
The Model of Nonprofit Organization Life Stages

Stage Five:
Review and Renew

Stage Four:
Produce and Sustain

Stage Three:
Ground and Grow

Stage Two:
Found and Frame

Stage One:
Imagine and Inspire

Decline and Dissolution

There are five nonprofit life stages. An organization can move into decline and dissolution from any one of those stages.

Assumptions about Nonprofit Organization Life Stages

The five stages are only part of the picture. To make use of the model, you need to understand how the stages interact with each other and the basis for the driving energy that pushes organizations forward. To that end, there are eight assumptions upon which this model rests:

1) Organizations are generally forward moving and the path and pace of the movement is predictable.

2) Organizations are multidimensional and the various dimensions interact to create a pattern unique to a particular life stage.

3) Five factors influence where an organization is at in its life cycle: age, size, growth rate of its field, social environment, and its primary leader's characteristics.

4) Significant events occur at each stage, and these are necessary to move an organization forward in its development.

5) There is not a predictable endpoint in organizational life.

6) There are distinct stages of an organization's life, but the boundaries between the stages aren't always obvious.

7) Each stage can be defined by dominant characteristics.

8) Each stage is uniquely valuable to the organization's positive development.

Let's look at each assumption in more detail.

1. *Organizations are generally forward moving and the path and pace of the movement is predictable.* While the speed at which organizations grow is somewhat predictable, unique organizational and environmental circumstances can cause organizations to move through stages faster or slower. At each stage there are opportunities for the organization to regress or progress. This opportunity for forward or backward movement is always present; however, the majority of organizations tend to develop at a relatively predictable gait.[2]

2. *Organizations are multidimensional and the various dimensions interact to create a pattern unique to a particular life stage.* This pattern is inevitable. Organizations must "begin" and with that beginning naturally comes advancement, setbacks, and challenges in certain identifiable ways. An analogy between human development and organization development best illustrates this point. Human beings, as with organizations, are complex creatures, and yet growth has been documented so that we can determine the health of an individual against a defined "normal" pattern of development. Healthy organization development can similarly be chronicled by assessing the patterns created by the various dimensions of organizational life.

Five factors influence where an organization is in its life cycle: age, size, growth rate of the industry, social environment, and leadership.

---

[2] Some reviewers of this book commented that we live in a time of fast-paced change with new organizational models emerging frequently. They suggested that the path and pace of organization development may not be as predictable as it once was.

3. *Five factors influence where an organization is at in its life cycle: age, size, growth rate of its field, social environment, and its primary leader's characteristics.* Based on the literature, several items are important to determining what life stage an organization is in.[3]

- *Age.* The chronological age of the organization may be an indication of its life cycle stage. For example, organizations one to three years old are typically in Stage Two: Found and Frame.

- *Size.* Organization size may be a clue to its life stage. For example, young organizations rarely have large numbers of staff whereas more mature organizations are more apt to.

- *Growth rate of the industry.* The particular field the organization is in may dictate that an organization matures more quickly. For example, in the 1980s the chemical dependency treatment industry grew very rapidly and was, for a time, quite profitable for both nonprofits and for-profits. Many such organizations passed through the early life stages quickly.

- *External environment.* Societal whims, market demand, technological changes, and cultural shifts may encourage some nonprofit organizations to speed through life stages. A good example of this involves the nonprofit response to the AIDS epidemic. The acknowledgment and urgency of addressing AIDS encouraged nonprofit organizations focusing on AIDS to spring up overnight.

- *Primary leader characteristics.* In a study of for-profit organizations Smith, Mitchell, and Summer found that the career stage of the organizational leader was a factor in organization development. They found, for example, that managers in the middle career stage show more concern for organization coordination, performance of the total organization, and strategic thinking. The skills, abilities, and personal style of the primary leader also influence the developmental cycle of organizations. For example, founders are sometimes excellent at creation but lack the skills to manage well; failure to find a different kind of leader with the required skills can affect development.[4]

4. *Significant events occur in each stage, and these events are necessary to move an organization forward in its development.* The occurrence of significant, and sometimes critical, events (such as the hiring of the first executive director or the loss of a major funder) within each stage help to identify that the organization is indeed in that stage, but also help the organization to move to the next stage. The organization's life will not progress forward if it does not encounter these "bumps." These junctures are essential to understanding the model.

5. *There is not a predictable end point in organizational life.* Once the organization

The career stage of the leader is a key factor influencing the organization's development.

---

[3] The work of Adizes (1979), Greiner (1972), and Lundberg (1986) supports this point.

[4] Hambrick and Crozier (1985) speak to this phenomenon directly.

has matured it reaches a point where internal or external realities will result in a mandate to change. This point may come quickly once the organization matures, or it may come decades later. Once at this point, however, the organization essentially follows one of two routes: it either addresses its challenges by rejuvenating to some extent (Stage Five: Review and Renew) or by dissolving into ineffectiveness (Decline and Dissolution). Therefore, while the life of nonprofit organizations is basically linear, it does not have a definitive end. At some point the organization chooses to remain status quo, stagnate, regenerate, or dissolve.

6. *There are distinct stages of an organization's life, but the boundaries between the stages aren't always obvious.* In real life, the stages may blur together far more than the model depicts. Organizations may have components of many different stages at once. Yet, when the whole organizational picture is painted, it can usually be placed in a particular stage.

7. *Each stage can be defined by dominant characteristics.* It is helpful to name predominant factors occurring in the organization at each stage. While the model distinguishes dominant organizational characteristics in each stage, real organizational life may not display these characteristics so neatly segmented.

8. *Each stage is uniquely valuable to the organization's positive development.* As mentioned previously, each stage consists of significant junctures. The people involved in these junctures often see them as negative occurrences. A basic assumption of the model is that each stage has both positive and negative aspects. Challenges and opportunities coexist as organizations grow. Whether the organization is changing via survival reaction or proactive action, the positive value of each stage should be recognized.

The Intertwined Arenas of Organizational Life

Organizations, like human beings, are complex entities. There are seven intertwined *arenas* that create this complexity, and it is the interplay of these arenas that characterize what stage of the life cycle an organization is in. The seven arenas of nonprofit organization life are governance, staff leadership, financing, administrative systems, staffing, products and services, and marketing. Figure 2, Seven Arenas of Nonprofit Organizations, on page 12, illustrates the arenas. Explanations of each arena follow.

Governance. Governance is defined as the board of directors and the processes and procedures. The board is the legal entity that oversees the nonprofit organization. The governing board of directors is the legal authority responsible for guarding the organization's adherence to its mission and ensuring its long-term stability and operations in order to do so. The board provides systematic linkages with other organizations and society at large. The board of directors establishes the strategic direction of the nonprofit in accordance with the needs of the community and expectations of the group that it serves. It regularly examines the agency's products and services to ensure that they fulfill the mission of the agency and achieve its objectives. The board sets broad level policies for the organization and plays a major role in fundraising. As an organization moves from stage to stage, the governance of the organization undergoes significant changes.

Staff leadership. In the nonprofit sector, the staff leadership role usually resides in a position titled "executive director." The executive director reports to the board of directors. The executive director is responsible for overseeing the operations of the organization, managing the human and financial resources, providing effective linkages with the community, and making day-to-day decisions on behalf of the organization. Changes in the role (and sometimes the person) of the executive director are related to life cycle stages.

Financing. Financing is the resource development and financial management arena of the nonprofit sector. Nonprofit organizations raise money through grants, fundraising events, service fees, private donations, endowments, planned giving, and service contracts. Financing usually becomes more complex, sophisticated, and secure as an organization matures.

Administrative systems. Administrative systems are the facilities and human resource management functions of the organization. These consist of the people, processes, and equipment the organization installs to manage its operations. Some administrative elements of the nonprofit organization are technology, accounting, support staff, office space, and evaluation functions. An organization's administrative systems increase in size and complexity as it moves from stage to stage in its life cycle.

Products and services. The products and services dimension of a nonprofit organization includes all those services the organization provides to accomplish its mission. The structure of a nonprofit organization often is defined by its program areas, products, and services. As the organization grows, the design and delivery of its activities transforms in accordance with that growth.

Staffing. How many people the organization employs, the number of paid and nonpaid employees, and the organizational structure used to delineate the relationships between employees are all components of this arena. One key to an organization's life cycle stage is the size and composition of its staff.

Marketing. Nonprofit organizations must let the public know what they can provide. A simple definition of marketing is that it "… is a process that helps you exchange something of value for something you need."[5] How the organization portrays itself (image), relates to the community (public relations), and becomes known to its customers (promotion) are all aspects of the organization's marketing. In the nonprofit sector marketing functions are often closely aligned with fundraising goals and activities. The presence and sophistication of marketing are signs of an organization's life stage.

Figure 2. Seven Arenas of Nonprofit Organizations

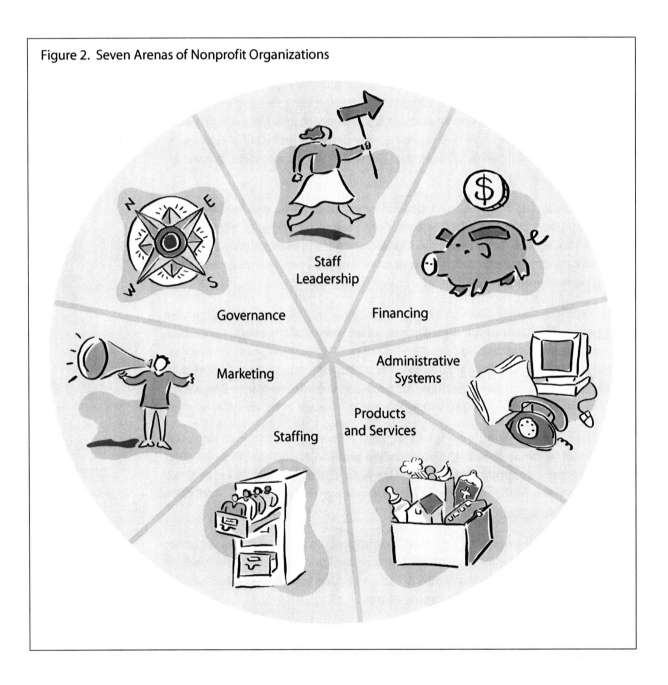

---

[5] Stern (2001, 4).

Obstacles and Opportunities along the Way

Each stage also can be characterized by obstacles and opportunities. Following is a definition of what is meant by these terms.

Obstacles. These are the critical factors and incidents within each stage, primarily internal to the organization, that can hinder an organization from developing successfully. Obstacles are the challenges and problems inherent in each stage. Often they must be acknowledged and addressed in order for the organization to progress. These are the "critical events" noted previously.

Opportunities. These are the positive aspects of the organizational systems that can aid the organization in continuing its successful development. They are the strengths embedded in each stage. If they are acknowledged and acted on they can greatly enhance the organization's development.

Table 6, Obstacles and Opportunities of Nonprofit Organization Life Cycle Stages, on page 44, summarizes these factors for each stage.

The Stages in Depth

Now that you have a big picture of the model, let's look at the stages in more detail. Nonprofit organizations typically progress through five stages. The first four stages are most predictable—that is, organizations are very likely to move through all of the first four stages. Stage Five is also evolutionary and inevitable, though it may take organizations a long time to reach it. Some organizations remain at Stage Four for decades without finding a need to reinvent themselves. The following section describes each stage in terms of organization arenas, highlights typical obstacles and opportunities, and offers tips for moving through the stage.

Stage One: Imagine and Inspire

Stage One is really the "twinkle in the eye" stage of a nonprofit organization's development. The organization is not yet formalized, let alone a nonprofit, tax exempt organization. Stage One is the period of the organization's life when a good idea is brewing in the minds of the founders. They believe they have a worthwhile concept of how to serve the common good and want to see their vision become a reality. The primary question facing the organization in this stage is, "Can this dream be realized?" Many more people will need to join to move the dream to a working idea. Organizations may remain in this stage for several years.

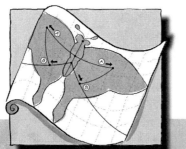

Table 1.

Stage One: Imagine and Inspire

Primary Question	Can this dream be realized?
Governance	Not yet a concern
Staff Leadership	Entrepreneurial, visionary, no positional leader, often volunteer
Financing	Not yet a concern
Administrative Systems	Not yet a concern
Staffing	Not yet a concern
Products and Services	Extremely informal or not yet a concern
Marketing	Not yet a concern
Obstacles	Fear of formalizing, lack of funding, no outside support
Opportunities	Creativity and energy of the dream, attracting new people to the dream
Duration of Stage	0–5 years

The arenas of the organization in Stage One are simple because it has not formally organized. There are no governance structures, financing, staff, products and services, or marketing. People join the cause, volunteering time and energy because they are friends of the founder or founders. The leaders are typically entrepreneurial and visionary, and viewed by others as self-confident.

Obstacles and opportunities

Obstacles

The greatest obstacles to organizational development at this stage include resistance to formalizing, lack of funding, and lack of expertise. The "organization" is built on the dreams of a characteristically visionary individual or small group of founders who tend to resist formal systems and external rules. These founders are often more skilled at imagining the possibilities than making the dreams reality. They often lack either the work style or the experience to focus on the formalizing steps. Likewise there is little financial or personnel support from other people to help the "idea" take form.

Opportunities

The joy of an organization in Stage One is the energy and enthusiasm of its founders. If the vision is compelling enough to inspire others to get involved, the organization will likely acquire the human and financial resources needed to form an official nonprofit entity.

Table 1: Stage One: Imagine and Inspire, above, summarizes the features of organizations in Stage One.

Case Study

The Little Theater Company that Could—and Did!

The following case study is included to provide a running example throughout this chapter of how a particular organization followed the five-stage path of development. It exemplifies each of the stages well at several points and deviates slightly at others—as will any organization. Joan Wells, executive director of Resources and Counseling for the Arts, developed the case study based on her many years of experience with arts organizations. The story combines elements of several organizations with which she has consulted. The identities of actual organizations and staff have been masked. It is the story of an organization that starts with a dream, grows, goes through significant changes, grows some more, reinvents itself, and in doing so, returns to an earlier point in its developmental path, poised to grow again in a new and different way. In the language of the model, it progresses from Stage One through Stage Five, then recycles back to Stage Four. Presumably it will find itself travelling the complete path of Stages Four and Five again in the future.

Imagine and Inspire

When the Little Theater Company (LTC) first opened in the fall of 1975 there was nothing to suggest it would be any different from the myriad of small theater companies that opened throughout the country that year. Yes, there was passion to produce dramatic productions that stretched the limits of theatrical possibilities. Yes, the artists were committed to doing work that included drama, music, movement, and visual art to provoke and stimulate audiences. Yes, everyone involved was determined to use theater to change society—to create socially significant art and address social issues like racism and war. But literally hundreds of other small groups of theater artists and musicians elsewhere shared that dream, and LTC didn't really seem all that different from the rest.

As it turned out, what was different about LTC was the caliber of the artists and their productions, and the zeal and stamina of the founding artistic director, Frank Smith. He was articulate and charismatic, and soon had attracted a broad following in both the theater community and the local theater aficionados, some of whom were wealthy and philanthropic.

After a year or so of putting on productions in schools, churches, and on rented stages, Smith and his cohorts decided that they had a large enough following and sufficient clarity of mission to establish themselves as a permanent fixture on the arts scene.

Signs of Stage One

Imagination and inspiration are quite evident in the dream of a theater that "stretches the limits of theatrical possibilities." The energy and stamina of the founding artistic director enables the dream to become reality. Many people enroll to help carry out the vision.

Tips for moving through Stage One

Overall Question	*Can this dream be realized?*
Overall Approach	*At this stage, keepers of the idea need to decide if it is worthwhile to pursue becoming a nonprofit organization.*

Governance
- Begin to locate people who will serve on the board.
- Review information on how to start a board.
- Draft articles of incorporation and bylaws.
- Secure a source of legal expertise.

Staff Leadership
- Find someone who has the time, energy, and skills to accomplish the necessary tasks to formalize the organization.

Financing
- Scout potential funding sources.
- Develop a business plan that outlines costs and revenue needed.
- Develop a fundraising plan.

Administrative Systems
- Identify possible administrative needs; include these in the concept paper and business plan.
- Decide where you will be housed.
- Locate a source of accounting expertise.
- Determine compliance requirements.

Staffing
- Identify short-term (one to two years) and long-term (two to four years) staffing needs.
- Generate alternate scenarios for filling staffing needs (volunteers, interns, part-time staff, contracted personnel).
- Develop a rudimentary orientation plan for staff.

Products and Services
- Consider different product or service options.
- Develop a concept paper to flesh out program ideas.
- Identify results you want to achieve.

Marketing
- Create a name for the concept and test it with various audiences.
- Generate interest and enthusiasm for the concept.
- Verify need and potential demand in target market.
- Use the concept paper to help "sell" the ideas.
- Identify initial marketing and promotional needs.

Stage Two: Found and Frame

An organization can be classified in Stage Two when it legally forms as a nonprofit entity. In Stage Two, the dreams and visions of Stage One assume a structure through which they can be achieved. The primary question arising for the organization in this stage is, "How are we going to pull this off?" The founder or founders now realize that making the dream a reality is going to require a lot of work and resources. They work hard to get the resources that will help them frame the organization. Organizations typically remain in this stage one to two years.

Arenas

Governance

In Stage Two a formal governance structure is created; the formation of a board of directors is a legal requirement. Typically the board of a newly formed Stage Two organization is small (three or four people), homogeneous, passionate about the mission of the organization, and geared for action. The people on this newly created board are not particularly interested in "governing" the organization, but are interested in seeing it come alive. They are highly motivated and willing to get involved at any level in order to bring the dream of the organization and what it can accomplish to fruition. Often the board members include the founder or founders of the organization.

Staff leadership

Staff leadership in a Stage Two organization is focused and driven. The staff leader may be called "co-ordinator" or "executive director" and may be paid or volunteer. Whether or not the staff leader was the original founder, the individual is typically visionary, entrepreneurial, and charismatic. The staff leader has a high degree of personal power and a large network of relationships. The staff leader in a Stage Two organization is comfortable being the sole decision maker and generally leads through autonomous rule.

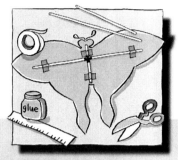

Table 2.
Stage Two: Found and Frame

Primary Question	How are we going to pull this off?
Governance	Formal governance structure created, homogenous, small, passionate board of directors, working board
Staff Leadership	Single-minded, driven, sole decision maker, visionary, entrepreneurial, charismatic
Financing	Start-up funding granted, limited funds, no accounting systems, in-kind donations of expertise
Administrative Systems	Few formal systems, a home office, small and agile
Staffing	Dedicated group of volunteers, no paid staff
Products and Services	One primary activity or a mix of varied, loosely related activities
Marketing	Word of mouth, no formal marketing
Obstacles	Fear of formalizing, reactive leadership
Opportunities	Excitement of funders, people wanting to join the organization, charismatic leader
Duration of Stage	1–2 years

Financing

Once the organization is serious about forming, financial resources begin to appear. Start-up funding is often granted by a community or corporate foundation intrigued with the organization's vision. These funds pay for many of the start-up costs including legal advice needed to form a nonprofit organization. While some financial resources become available to the organization, there are also many in-kind donations made to the organization, including donations of legal or program advice. Even though money is beginning to trickle into the organization, the nonprofit is not sophisticated enough at this stage to have sound financial accounting systems. Often a simple, first-time budget is prepared. Obtaining a fiscal agent or operating under the wing of a more established 501(c)(3) is normal in this stage. Even with initial start-up funding, the organization has very limited funds.

Administrative systems

It is easy to spot a nonprofit organization in Stage Two: They often operate out of the founder's home with very few formal administrative systems. Procedures and clear systems of communication are nearly nonexistent. Administrative details get tended to informally, if at all. This lack of systems and structure works well for the organization at this stage because it is small and agile.

Staffing

Stage Two is accomplished by a dedicated group of volunteers who are essential to helping the organization realize its goals and are willing to do whatever needs to be done in order for the organization to thrive. These volunteers are most likely personal friends of the founder or board. There are usually no paid staff and no job descriptions. There are no (or few) systems of accountability, no formal organizational structure, and no defined communication channels.

Products and services

The mission of the organization *is* its products and services. Usually, the new nonprofit has not yet defined how it is going to carry out its mission and therefore is doing either one focused activity or is involved in a myriad of activities loosely tied to the organization's stated mission. These activities are often short range.

Marketing

The typical Stage Two organization becomes known via word of mouth. There is no formal vehicle to inform the public that the organization exists.

Obstacles and opportunities

Obstacles

Many of the same obstacles confront an organization in Stage Two as in Stage One. Founders may fear formalizing the organization, believing it will compromise the vision. The ability to lay the foundation for the organization may be inhibited by the difficulty in corralling the entrepreneurial, high-energy, visionary nature of the founders or the challenge of sustaining the enthusiasm and interest of volunteers.

Opportunities

Creating a new organization is very exciting for all involved. Stage Two's strength is that it is fast moving and inspirational. People *want* to join the organization and see it fulfill its mission. Funders are excited about the organization's prospects. The charismatic leader of a Stage Two organization can be a tremendous asset to an organization.

Table 2: Stage Two: Found and Frame, on page 17, summarizes the features of a Stage Two organization.

Case Study

Found and Frame

Following weeks of meetings and intense discussions, the large group of interested people divided themselves into two groups—one would become the official "board of directors" and the other an "artistic advisory board." Most of the actors, directors, producers, and others whose interest and talent lay in theatrical production assigned themselves to the artistic advisory panel. The board of directors included people with the necessary interests, skills, and connections: two lawyers, a banker, an architect, two marketing executives, and three or four community volunteers who were well connected in the philanthropic community.

The members of the board immediately filed articles of incorporation and applied for a tax-exempt ruling that made LTC a charitable organization. One of the first things the board did was to make personal pledges to enable the fledgling theater to establish a line of credit at a local bank.

The board also began considering the possibility of buying a local movie theater that had begun as a vaudeville stage. It needed considerable renovation but could be returned to its former charm. Dressing rooms and a tack room were added, and there was space in an adjacent building for a set shop. Of course, the artistic staff was delighted with the idea of a permanent "home" and eagerly joined in the planning.

At the same time, LTC's artistic work continued. The company garnered impressive reviews in the local press, with particular mention of the professionalism of the actors, the high quality of sets and costumes, and the overall enjoyment generated by an evening at the theater. The excellence of the artistic work and the enthusiasm of the exceptional board of directors recruited by Frank Smith soon made LTC the one arts group in town with which everyone wanted to be associated.

Signs of Stage Two

The organization takes the steps to incorporate. The artistic director personally recruits the members of the board of directors. The physical space is less than ideal. The organization is operating on a shoestring budget with minimal broad-based support.

Tips for moving through Stage Two

Overall Question	*How are we going to pull this off?*
Overall Approach	*Prioritize a few key organizational items to focus on. Most likely to need attention are resource development, basic administrative procedures, and development of quality programs or services.*

Governance
- Create a formal governance structure.
- Expand the board.
- Offer board training on basic board roles and responsibilities.

Staff Leadership
- Provide a mentor or coach for the lead staff person.
- Address the lead staff person's leadership weaknesses through skill building or hiring of additional staff.

Financing
- Expand the funding base.
- Institute standard accounting practices and procedures.
- Strategize for future financial needs.

Administrative Systems
- Establish an office.
- Formalize record keeping and filing.

Staffing
- Use volunteers effectively.
- Recognize the dedication of volunteers.
- Anticipate staffing needs.
- Hire administrative support.
- Consider contract or part-time staff.

Products and Services
- Assess and improve the quality of products and services.
- Begin to define criteria for which activities to pursue and which to table.

Marketing
- Develop a fact sheet.
- Develop contacts with volunteer recruiting sources.
- Develop an organization identity: logo, mission, vision, values, slogan, or tagline.

Stage Three: Ground and Grow

During Stage Three the nonprofit is defining and expanding itself as an entity. It has the energy of youth but also some wisdom gained through its early years of formation. It sees the path toward achieving its vision and wants to traverse it. Opportunities to build and grow are numerous, but so are the demands for administrative accountability. The primary question facing the organization in this stage is "How can we build this to be viable?" It is perhaps the most exciting time in the organization's life, but also requires the most growth in many organizational arenas. Most organizations live in Stage Three for two to five years.

Arenas

Governance

The initial group of three or four people who were mustered to obtain nonprofit status in Stage Two expands in a Stage Three organization. The original passionate and personally acquainted core group of board members now must consider enlarging their numbers to meet the demands of the growing organization and the requirements of funders. For perhaps the first time in the life of the organization outsiders are brought into the organization—people who do not have personal ties to the founder and who are being recruited to the organization for their expertise rather than solely for their passion for the organization's mission. Legal and accounting experts are common examples of this phenomenon. The organization is still governed rather loosely and is more reliant on the leader's zeal than on important board-led decisions. The governance role of the board remains primarily reactionary, setting policies and considering long-term issues for the organization only in response to some immediate need. In this stage they are often still a "working" board, providing lots of volunteer support in the day-to-day activities.

Table 3.
Stage Three: Ground and Grow

Primary Question	How can we build this to be viable?
Governance	Expansion of the board size, first "outsider" on board, reactive rather than strategic
Staff Leadership	First paid executive director, who is directive, unavailable, high-energy, needed both internally and externally
Financing	Greater need for financial resources, a few funder relationships established, proficient use of in-kind donations, discussion of revenue-generating schemes
Administrative Systems	High need for administrative systems, first office space rented, first administrative staff hired, systems of accountability developed, technology and equipment purchased
Staffing	Paid staff hired, volunteers still critical part of staffing strategy, lack of job descriptions
Products and Services	One primary activity, refinement in program delivery, need to say "no" to program ideas due to lack of resources
Marketing	Fact sheet or first brochure developed, word of mouth still primary marketing avenue
Obstacles	Absence of systems of accountability, overwhelmed with new elements entering the organizational system, danger in remaining an isolated system
Opportunities	Sense of accomplishment, creating a flexible, innovative organization receptive to change, diversification of the agency
Duration of Stage	2–5 years

Staff leadership

In a Stage Three organization a paid executive director position is usually created. The executive director tends to lead staff in a directive manner based on personal relationships. The executive director is the "pulse" of the Stage Three organization, making most of the primary decisions. He or she is pulled in myriad directions as the organization struggles to meet all of its obligations. Staff and board may find the executive director inaccessible in this stage and yet critical to the organization's functioning. Often, the executive director must attend to an enlarged internal role as well as an expanded external role.

Financing

In a Stage Three organization funds are flowing more steadily to the organization. Simultaneously the organization's need for financial resources is considerably greater than in previous stages. The nonprofit begins to cultivate relationships with specific funders and generate more defined financing strategies. The organization begins to feel confident that funds will be forthcoming from a certain number of these sources. A more sophisticated budget is prepared to assist the organization in anticipating its spending patterns and income flow. The organization is now fairly proficient at capitalizing on its volunteer resources and garners many in-kind donations. Even with increased ability to solicit in-kind donations and solidify funder relationships, the organization's financial needs are just barely being met. Staff and board are discussing, for the first time, how to *generate* revenue to increase income and meet rising administrative and future expenses. No longer can the organization rely solely on in-kind donations and start-up grants.

Administrative systems

The need for administrative systems heightens significantly for the nonprofit in Stage Three. With increased revenue and more demand for service, the home-based office is no longer functional. Nonprofit organizations in Stage Three often rent their first office space and hire their first administrative staff person. As the organization expands, so does its need for systems of accountability. Financial accounting systems and more sophisticated budgeting are implemented. At the same time, technological aids and office equipment are purchased.

Staffing

The crux of Stage Three is the need for additional staff to keep up with the organization's expansion. With funding in place, an office, and clarity of mission, the organization is ready to hire staff. A Stage Three organization rarely has job descriptions, salary structures, and personnel policies in place, but the newly acquired staff is content with the informal nature of the organization. Staff members join a Stage Three organization because they are driven by the organization's mission, not because they feel that they will be compensated greatly for their expertise. Volunteers are often an integral part of the staffing strategy, doing much of the work that one would find paid staff doing in a more mature organization. For this reason, volunteer recruitment, orientation, recognition, and retention are common activities.

Products and services

The products and services provided by an organization in Stage Three are similar to those provided in Stage Two. If the organization is offering one primary program, some refinements in that program occur in Stage Three as the organization gets more proficient and efficient in its delivery of services. If the organization is engaged in a number of activities, loosely connected to its mission, it begins to be more strategic and narrow in its focus. The challenge for a Stage Three organization is to keep up with the demand for service generated by the public's awareness of the new agency. For the first time, the board and executive director need to say "no" to some program ideas because the organization does not have the capacity to implement them or has learned that certain approaches yield greater impact than others.

Marketing

A Stage Three organization is now in a position to develop its first official promotional tool. Often this is a fact sheet or simple brochure that introduces the organization and tells about its broad mission. This promotional tool is developed in response to requests for information about the agency by potential funders, potential volunteers, new board members, and potential new customers or clients. Most people continue to learn about the agency through word of mouth. A planned and concerted marketing effort by a Stage Three organization is rare.

Obstacles and opportunities

Obstacles

A Stage Three organization is expanding in a variety of ways and therefore introducing many new elements to the organizational system. Stage Three organizations can become nervous about all these new elements and may either resist or simply not have the financial or human resources to implement changes and innovations. This limits the organization's ability to progress. In the same vein, some Stage Three organizations are unable or unwilling to implement accountability systems or broaden their base of volunteers. Lack of adequate human resources and organizational systems combined with increased demand and visibility results in organizational chaos. This chaos may quickly alienate funders, clients, volunteers, and staff.

Opportunities

There are many rewards for an organization in Stage Three. Board and funders feel an enormous sense of accomplishment as the organization establishes more definite systems and procedures. As the products and services improve, clients benefit. New faces and new voices on the board and staff bring new ideas and new energy. This can rejuvenate the founders, who are tired from the hard work expended to get the organization established.

Table 3: Stage Three: Ground and Grow, on page 21, summarizes the characteristics of Stage Three organizations.

Case Study

Ground and Grow

Fundraising for the theater renovations went surprisingly smooth. Construction moved along without undue delays, and when the curtain went up on opening night of the first production every seat in the house was full, at least until the standing ovation that ended the evening.

Smith and his company and the board of directors were naturally ecstatic, despite the fatigue that invariably follows such a massive effort as carrying out a capital campaign and putting on a show at the same time. Everyone involved felt satisfied and even just a little bit smug! They looked forward to many seasons of great plays in their wonderful new playhouse.

There were a few unanticipated problems with the building, of course. The first winter the pipes in the basement froze during an unusual cold snap; and snow removal was erratic and expensive. In the summer the theater was usually closed because the cost of air conditioning was exorbitantly high. This was a big disappointment, for the company had hoped to offer theater classes to high school students in the summer to help defray some of the operating expenses.

Signs of Stage Three

Fundraising comes easily. There are hints that some funder relationships are being established. Pressures on the limited budget are evident, especially related to operational expenses. Word-of-mouth advertising is successful.

Tips for moving through Stage Three

Overall Question	*How can we build this organization to be viable?*
Overall Approach	*In general, focus on actions that will prepare the organization for a stable and secure future.*

Governance
- Systematize the board recruitment process.
- Offer board training.
- Initiate annual board retreats to build the board's effectiveness in its role.
- Develop board policies and train the board to focus on its policy role.

Staff Leadership
- Clarify executive director's primary roles, responsibilities, and accountabilities.
- Ease the executive director's responsibilities through delegation and addition of staff.

Financing
- Develop a multiyear budget.
- Create a fundraising plan.

Administrative Systems
- Hire administrative support staff.
- Develop administrative and financial policies and procedures.
- Incorporate automated data management systems including administrative, financial, and client data.
- Purchase necessary technology and equipment.

Staffing
- Hire program staff.
- Expand volunteer base.
- Develop job descriptions and organization charts.
- Refine volunteer management functions.

Products and Services
- Develop strategic plan to clarify where the organization is going with products and services and how they interrelate.
- Identify client outcomes and methods for measuring and analyzing them.

Marketing
- Develop an organization image and promotional tools.

Stage Four: Produce and Sustain

The Stage Four organization is in its prime. It is productive, well established, feels secure in its structure and services, and is a recognized player in its field. Generally people feel good about the organization. The organization is stable and provides worthwhile services. The primary question arising for the organization in this stage is, "How can we sustain the momentum?" While the mission has remained relatively constant since the organization was formed, the established Stage Four organization has a reputation among agencies, funders, and clients as a successful provider of a wide range of services. A Stage Four organization has all the systems in place to support greater services, yet they want to remain true to their mission and not get spread too thin. This is often the stage at which an organization engages in its first truly *comprehensive* strategic planning process. Organizations may have their longest tenure in this stage—they may remain in it for as short as seven years or as long as thirty. For this reason an early Stage Four organization may have some significant differences from a late Stage Four organization. For example, the board of an early Stage Four organization may have no committees and set few policies, whereas a late Stage Four organization board may have several active committees and view its role primarily as policy governance. Likewise, an early Stage Four organization may have extremely stable and reliable funding, but a later Stage Four organization must seriously explore new sources of funding.

Table 4.

Stage Four: Produce and Sustain

Primary Question	How can we sustain the momentum?
Governance	The governing role is in its prime, few founding board members remain, board discussions broadly focused, well-developed committees, board role is to ensure well-being and longevity of the organization, board-staff roles clearly defined, diverse composition
Staff Leadership	Well-rounded executive director, needs good delegation skills, assistant director in place, complemented by good program managers, "founder's syndrome" may be present
Financing	Stable funding, development of an operating reserve, need for exploration of new and expanded funding sources, fundraiser position added
Administrative Systems	In their prime, policies and procedures are well-developed, multiple support staff, revamping of hardware and software
Staffing	Organization size is at its peak, program managers hired, increased diversity of staff, volunteer structure self-perpetuating, volunteer coordinator hired, first staff firing may occur
Products and Services	Programs well-designed and functioning at high level, long-range program planning, core programs secure but new programs being tried, many opportunities for expansion
Marketing	Sophisticated marketing efforts, professional image, marketing plan developed, organization expands beyond word-of-mouth promotion
Obstacles	Lack of control or too much control by organizational leadership, lack of risk-taking, organizational stagnation, board unable to move to a governing role, board focuses too much on day-to-day operations
Opportunities	Feeling of security, adequate human and financial resources, new staff and board brings fresh ideas
Duration of Stage	7–30 years

Arenas

Governance

The board of a Stage Four organization is also in its prime. At this point in the organization's life, the board has had a great deal of turnover and may find that there are few founding members left on the board. This significant difference from earlier years allows the board to have a broader focus. Also, the size and stability of the organization at this stage enables the board to assume a true governance function and structure. Stage Four boards have a well-developed committee structure. They discuss policy, strategic direction, and organizational vision during board meetings. The board members perceive their jobs as ensuring the well-being and longevity of the organization so that it can continue to fulfill its mission and service to the community. The board and the executive director are clear about lines of authority and responsibility. There is a commitment by both to shared power and authority. In the years since the organization's inception the board has expanded and now represents a healthy diversity.

Staff leadership

The executive director is still the primary staff leader in a Stage Four organization, but is complemented by a number of well-qualified managers. Because of the size and complexity of the organization at this stage, an assistant director is often brought into the organization. The executive director has thorough knowledge of the organization—both operations and programs—and is a well-rounded, capable communicator. To be effective at this stage, the executive director needs good management skills, including the ability to delegate. A significant source of conflict may be present for the organization if either the executive director is the organization's founder or there are original founding members on the board. In Stage Four, the organization is being pushed to expand beyond its original boundaries, hopes, and dreams, and this may conflict with those founding members. This is one of the signs of what is often referred to as the "founder's syndrome."

Financing

One of the reasons a Stage Four organization is in its prime is that its financing is relatively stable. It has a steady cash flow, adequate accounting systems, and an efficient budgeting process. Stage Four organizations often have enough reliable sources of funding, programs and services well integrated into the community that the organization's leadership may consider creating an operating reserve to safeguard the organization's future. While many funding streams are reliable, expansion of staff, programs, and administrative activities requires that the organization explore new and expanded sources of funding. Additional administrative expenses, such as the establishment of pension plans and outlay of capital expenses, help to ensure the prosperity of the organization but also demand greater resources. The position of a fundraiser is often added to the payroll in Stage Four. As well, it is at this stage that the loss or gain of a big grant will significantly impact the organization.

Administrative systems

Administrative systems are in their heyday in a Stage Four organization. The organization has written—and uses—personnel policies, salary schedules, annual performance reviews, and formal job descriptions. There is a well-defined client record system. Evaluation of programs is an ongoing function. In contrast to a Stage Two organization which has only one administrative staff person (if at all), the Stage Four organization has multiple support staff. The computers that were begged and borrowed to help the organization in its start-up phase are replaced with state-of-the-art hardware and software. In Stage Four, funders and staff members are pleased with the administrative systems in place to help the organization focus on its mission.

Staffing

The number of employees is at its peak in a Stage Four organization. Many have specialized functions. There is a self-perpetuating volunteer structure. Program managers have been hired or promoted from within to assist with the increased personnel and ensure high-quality services. Just as with the board in a Stage Four organization, the increase in staff brings new and diverse people to the organization. This diversity is generally welcomed but can be a source of conflict with staff members who joined the organization early on. The organization in Stage Four often faces its first instance of firing a staff member. In addition to a fundraiser, a volunteer coordinator is often hired to manage the growing sophistication and scope of the volunteer activities.

Products and services

Programs in a Stage Four organization are well designed, results oriented, and client focused. Some of the more established activities undergo review to ensure that the quality is still high. The addition of specialized staff and program managers encourages the organization to increase its long-range program planning. While core programs in Stage Four continue with relative security, the organization starts many new programs. The increased visibility and capacity of the organization invites numerous opportunities for program expansion. Staff and board of the nonprofit organization need to wrestle with these invitations to expand.

Marketing

The marketing in a Stage Four organization becomes much more sophisticated. The organization has developed a professional image complete with a logo, tagline, and well-designed brochure. Marketing publications such as annual reports and newsletters are regularly distributed. The need to attract more clients and more dollars to sustain the organization encourages the organization to develop a marketing plan. Word of mouth is still a useful marketing tool, but the organization no longer relies on it as its only promotional mechanism.

Obstacles and opportunities

Obstacles

The barriers in the Produce and Sustain stage are inherent in its size and complexity. The leadership may exhibit lack of control or too much control; either extreme causes tremendous turmoil. There can be very difficult communication challenges between staff and board or between and among staff members. The stability of Stage Four can also lull the organization into complacency and stagnation, discouraging risk taking and creativity, both of which are needed for the organization to continue to be vibrant. An influx of new staff and board members may result in conflicts between the new and old guard. Problematic boards in Stage Four organizations are usually those who have not been able to distinguish themselves as a governing rather than a working board. Some Stage Four boards get far too consumed with the day-to-day operations and hinder the organization's functioning.

Opportunities

Working in a Stage Four nonprofit organization can be very rewarding. The organization is known by many and feels like a secure place to work; employees and volunteers like being identified with the organization. There are enough human and financial resources for the organization to take some risks and try some new things. The influx of new staff and board bring new ideas and new possibilities to a Stage Four organization.

Table 4: Stage Four: Produce and Sustain, on page 26, summarizes the key characteristics of a Stage Four organization.

Case Study

Produce and Sustain

A few years went by, and there were many good plays and a few great productions. Many actors were "discovered" from the stage of LTC and lured off to the bad old Big Apple, but they always came back for cameo appearances or fundraisers; and there were always new, young faces eager for greasepaint and spotlights.

One of the "faces" to disappear from the theater was that of Frank Smith, who went off to the West Coast, where he became the head of an excellent university theater. The personnel committee, made up primarily of board members, soon hired a young director eager to make her mark on the community.

The established company had become accustomed to the reputation of being the best show in town. Plus it enjoyed the approbation it received for providing such a cultural opportunity. To be sure, after the first year audiences had dropped off somewhat, but "everyone" knew that this was bound to happen as the novelty wore off. No one seemed to be paying attention to this subtle decline.

Increasing costs (salaries, equity rates, energy costs, and just about everything else seemed to go up each year) and falling ticket sales were a deadly combination. At first, LTC tried to counter the growing deficit by increasing the price of tickets—which had the effect of decreasing ticket sales without increasing total income.

Signs of Stage Four

Successful plays are being produced and attended. One of the original founders, the artistic director, leaves the organization. Financial pressures mount as the administrative costs rise with the organization's growth.

Tips for moving through Stage Four

How can we sustain the momentum?

Overall Question	*Take steps that will stabilize the organization in the present, address any areas of tension or conflict that are emerging, and create security for the organization's future.*
Overall Approach	

Governance

- Formalize an executive director performance review process.
- Initiate an annual or biennial board self-assessment.
- Develop or revise the board committee structure.

Staff Leadership

- Implement and follow up on an executive director performance review to highlight potential areas of concern and opportunities for professional development.
- Clarify the executive director's primary roles, responsibilities, and accountabilities, especially in regard to management of staff.

Financing

- Develop an operating reserve.
- Review the fundraising plan and look for areas to expand.
- Consider hiring or contracting the fund development function.

Administrative Systems

- Upgrade hardware and software.
- Ensure administrative staffing levels are adequate.

Staffing

- Increase management personnel.
- Actively address issues arising from increased diversity of staff.
- Ensure that volunteer recruitment and retention are tended to.
- Hire a volunteer coordinator.
- Obtain legal counsel if staff firing is imminent.

Products and Services

- Develop long-range plans for products and services.
- Try out new program models and approaches.
- Develop an internal system for assessing and responding to new opportunities.

Marketing

- Develop a marketing plan.
- Define or reassess organization logo and image.

Stage Five: Review and Renew

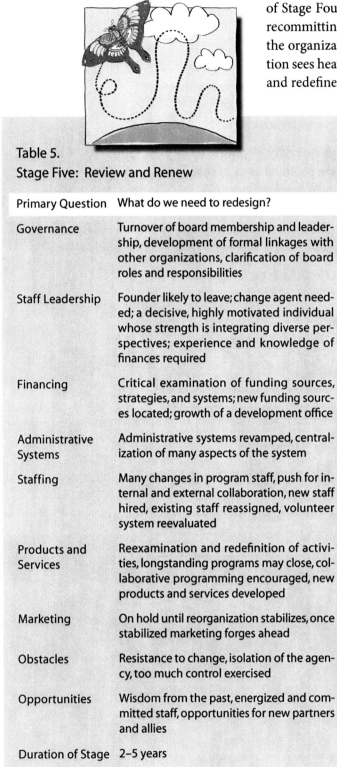

The Stage Five organization is responding to many of the obstacles of Stage Four (stagnation, lack of risk taking, staff conflicts) by recommitting to its mission and rejuvenating itself. As it does so, the organization feels renewed. Typically, a Stage Five organization sees heavy turnover in leadership at the board and staff levels and redefines many of its activities. The primary question facing the organization in this stage is, "What do we need to redesign?" The organization is trying to reconnect with its roots and revive the elements that helped it reach its prime. Because organizations are in the process of change, they typically want to move through it rather quickly and generally remain in this stage no more than a few years.

Arenas

Governance

A Stage Five organization's board often has to take giant steps to emerge anew. This may take the form of new board leadership, the creation of an almost entirely new board, or a renewed and vigorous level of commitment from board members. The board in a Stage Five organization strives to develop formal linkages with other organizations and recommits itself as stewards of the nonprofit and its mission. Some of the challenges that were faced in Stage Four such as conflict between the board and the executive director get resolved through clarifying or rethinking roles and responsibilities.

Staff leadership

The executive director of a Stage Five organization is rarely the same individual who was the executive director in earlier stages. Organizations in Stage Five need a director who is a change agent, someone who is decisive, highly motivated, and is viewed as an integrator. Re-

Table 5.
Stage Five: Review and Renew

Primary Question	What do we need to redesign?
Governance	Turnover of board membership and leadership, development of formal linkages with other organizations, clarification of board roles and responsibilities
Staff Leadership	Founder likely to leave; change agent needed; a decisive, highly motivated individual whose strength is integrating diverse perspectives; experience and knowledge of finances required
Financing	Critical examination of funding sources, strategies, and systems; new funding sources located; growth of a development office
Administrative Systems	Administrative systems revamped, centralization of many aspects of the system
Staffing	Many changes in program staff, push for internal and external collaboration, new staff hired, existing staff reassigned, volunteer system reevaluated
Products and Services	Reexamination and redefinition of activities, longstanding programs may close, collaborative programming encouraged, new products and services developed
Marketing	On hold until reorganization stabilizes, once stabilized marketing forges ahead
Obstacles	Resistance to change, isolation of the agency, too much control exercised
Opportunities	Wisdom from the past, energized and committed staff, opportunities for new partners and allies
Duration of Stage	2–5 years

generating requires all these skills. Additionally the staff of the organization needs a leader who is experienced and knowledgeable about finances. The exit of the founder from the agency (voluntarily or forcibly) is a key indicator that the organization is in the stage of Review and Renew.

Financing

A Stage Five organization looks critically at its funding sources, strategies, and systems. New funding sources are cultivated that support the organization's newly defined operational and programmatic efforts. Stage Five organizations often expand the development office so that the regeneration efforts succeed.

Administrative systems

Revamping significant parts of the administrative systems is often a primary activity in a Stage Five organization. Systems that have been in place for many years are revised and many aspects of the system are centralized to allow for greater control.

Staffing

Program-related staffing is where many of the greatest changes occur in a Stage Five organization. As the organization reexamines its mission and services and tries to resolve the challenges that were presented to it in Stage Four, resignations, firings, layoffs, and retirements among staff and volunteers seem to occur frequently. Additionally, staff is reorganized or asked to work more collaboratively with each other and with external agencies. The volunteer system may need revamping as well. New staff is hired to represent the agency's new direction. There is an identified distinction within the organization of veteran versus new staff members.

Products and services

In Stage Five, the organization reexamines, redefines, and experiments with programs, activities, and products. Longstanding programs may be closed or combined in new ways with other programs. Additionally, the organization initiates more collaborative approaches to providing service and develops products and programs that relate to the agency's mission in a new way.

Marketing

Little marketing is done in the early stages of the Review and Renew Stage. Self-examination and reorganization must occur before the organization can adequately market itself. It is as if an organizational makeover is occurring. After the makeover is complete, marketing efforts occur with a flurry as the agency hurries to communicate its new image and vision.

Obstacles and opportunities

Obstacles

Review and Renew requires an enormous amount of energy and trust by all connected to the agency. Efforts to stem the tide of change by staff or board can inhibit this energy. If the agency did not deal successfully with the challenges of Stage Four it may have become too isolated, too controlled, or too resistant to change to be able to make it through the revisions required for Stage Five.

Opportunities

The Stage Five organization has its organizational history as one of its strengths. Wisdom from the past will help guide the organization through this stage. A core group of energized and committed staff and board, fueled by excitement about the new direction, can contribute positively to the changes afoot. Organizations in the Review and Renew stage also have many opportunities to engage with others by finding new partners and allies to help them achieve their new vision.

Table 5: Stage Five: Review and Renew, on page 32, summarizes the key characteristics of an organization in the Review and Renew stage.

Case Study

Review and Renew

Members of the board of directors, always quick to take credit in good times, looked about for someone to blame for the problems, and their sights alighted upon the new artistic director. She, in the view of the board, was producing too many strange new works and not enough of the standard theater repertory that LTC had built its reputation and theater upon; and she wasn't controlling costs adequately.

Following an acrimonious, finger-pointing executive committee meeting, an advertisement for a new artistic director appeared in theater journals around the country. After an extensive search the board finally hired an experienced director from another city, who seemed likely to follow the board's instruction and put on plays that would appeal to the suburban, middle-class audiences that were expected to come to the theater.

By this time in LTC's life, most of the original company had departed for other venues, and the original board had been completely replaced. The mission that had imbued LTC with energy and vigor was nearly forgotten, and the bottom line (of the balance sheet) was the primary concern of the board. Members of the theatrical company—interested primarily in their own careers—and members of the board of directors had little in common, and no one remembered the common cause that had created LTC in the first place!

As the theater lurched into its next season, few reviews were appearing in the press, and those that did were less than laudatory. Reviewers frequently used terms like "old chestnuts" and "insipid," "lackluster," and "uninspiring" to describe the plays and performances. Audiences, as the saying goes, stayed away in droves.

In order to earn some income, LTC had been in the habit of renting space to other theater companies for their productions, and this was to be their salvation. One such company was the Phoenix Theater Company.

Phoenix was a vibrant, young company with a compelling mission of producing innovative new works, and an emphasis on artistic excellence, innovation, and risk-taking. Phoenix audiences were young and growing—it seemed obvious that the Phoenix Theater Company was on the upswing while LTC was going in the opposite direction.

Someone, somehow had the idea to merge the two companies and create a joint enterprise. This could update LTC's image and provide resources to Phoenix at lower cost, including guaranteed use of the stage, access to lights and costumes, and a scene shop. A marriage of convenience, so to speak, rather than one based on love and shared goals.

There were considerable reservations on both sides. The Phoenix company was concerned that LTC would try to control its creativity and some LTC board members feared that the Phoenix productions would offend what was left of the LTC audiences. But something had to be done and it seemed worth a try. For LTC the only other option was to sell the building and close the doors of the company.

After considerable discussion, including hiring a consultant skilled in managing mergers, the two companies were legally joined as New Joint Theater (NJT), and the difficult task of combining their very different cultures began. The director of the LTC retired—an act everyone felt spared the theater a difficult decision. Jane Black, the director of the Phoenix, was offered the position of director of NJT, and in spite of considerable reservations she accepted.

Signs of Stage Five

There is major disagreement between board and staff. Board actions verge on micro-management. Turmoil brews within the organization, requiring a significant change—in this case a merger. A large degree of staff turnover is happening. New blood rejuvenates the organization as the "younger" theater company enters the merger. Focus on revenue-producing strategies intensifies.

Tips for Moving through Stage Five

Overall Question	*What do we need to redesign?*
Overall Approach	*Review the internal and external strengths, weaknesses, opportunities, and threats to the organization. Determine where revitalization is most needed and develop a plan to implement changes so that the organization stays cutting edge.*

Governance
- Hold a board retreat to discuss and review board roles and responsibilities.
- Develop or revitalize the board nominating committee.
- Initiate discussions, do site visits, or bring in speakers who represent potential partners and new perspectives.

Staff Leadership
- Develop a succession plan for executive director and other key staff positions.
- Initiate a development plan for the executive director.
- Explore ways to focus the executive director's energies and utilize his or her strengths.
- Explore the organization's finances in-depth to uncover any vulnerability.

Financing
- Expand funding sources.
- Add staff to the development function.
- Analyze current funding strategies.

Administrative Systems
- Revamp administrative systems—equipment and structure.
- Centralize key administrative functions.

Staffing
- Review organization structure.
- Revamp or create a staff orientation program.
- Prepare for staff changes—staff leaving, new staff coming, staff taking on new positions.
- Consider new staffing structures such as job sharing, co-location of staff with other agencies, shared staff with other agencies.
- Create internal career development opportunities.

Products and Services
- Undertake a strategic planning process to review activities.
- Explore new collaborative relationships.[6]
- Actively seek best-practice service models.

Marketing
- Ensure that marketing goals are realistic.
- Slow down marketing efforts until major organization changes are completed.

---

[6] For guidance on collaborations, see Mattessich and Monsey (2001), and Winer and Ray (1994).

Case Study

Return to Produce and Sustain

Times continued to be tough for the theater, but Black was inspiring and the artists who remained with the company were visionary, dedicated, and hard-working. The Phoenix had gained the respect of many funders and donors, so there were some grants and contributions available—enough, at least, to continue operating the theater on a shoestring. And continue they did. In addition to stimulating audiences with one major production each year, the new company gave workshops and provided collaborative training to empower theater artists including actors, musicians, set and light designers and directors, whose understanding of what theater can be was stretched.

Black understood the need of the theater to operate in the black, and she showed savvy in her ability to build audiences. While retaining the creative direction of the theater herself, she hired a successful communications director and gave him a free hand in creating publicity and audience packages that seemed likely to fill the seats. Black's reputation as an artistic director grew in the arts community. The work of NJT improved in quality as innovative techniques were used for traditional plays, while contemporary work was also introduced. Black kept the company focused on its mission and on producing excellent work. Theater artists and musicians from around the country vied to work with the group.

Still NJT existed on a shoestring budget, and the lack of resources hampered growth and took its toll on the participants, especially the "administrators." The size of the board dropped to the legal minimum and Black began to realize that she needed to strengthen the administration, hire permanent staff, and build a funding program. Since her first love was with the art side of theater production, this seemed a formidable task, almost insurmountable.

Fortunately, Black had taken care to cultivate good relationships with several of the members of her board of directors. One of them introduced Black to several area funders, and she discovered that two were interested in helping small arts organizations—one by offering fellowships to arts administrators wanting to develop their skills, and a second by giving capital- and capacity-building grants to small and midsized nonprofits. Black applied for and won a fellowship, which allowed her to work with a mentor and create a strategic plan for NJT.

With the help of a local service agency that offered in-kind help to small nonprofits, Black developed a proposal to buy office equipment (two computers, a copier, and a printer), and to hire some administrative help, including an administrative assistant and a part-time bookkeeper. The addition of these vital staff positions and the help of her mentor, who was excited about the mission of the theater, alleviated much of the stress that Black was feeling and freed her to think of other creative ways for the company to work in the community.

continued

Eventually, NJT began to recruit new community board members. Care was taken that each new member understood and was committed to the mission of NJT, that he or she was prepared to advocate for the theater and to help raise money and locate other resources. In addition, each was expected to share his or her particular skills and talents with the organization. The strengthened board was able in a short time to find new funders, re-enlist current funders, and provide more help to the growing staff of New Joint Theater.

Because of the theater's increasing profile in the arts community, a couple who ran a local advertising agency saw an opportunity to increase their own visibility in the area by offering pro bono services to create a communications and marketing plan for NJT! Black made sure that the board members and staff understood their parts in promoting this offer, and she also made sure that the advertising company understood the mission and vision of the theater. It was truly a match made in heaven. The advertising firm was committed to innovative marketing and its work showed a theatrical flair.

With the strategic plan designed by Black, NJT anticipated the need for administrative structures that handled increased ticket sales, the demand for information, the need for contracts with artists, musicians, and performing spaces, and many other challenges that beset a successful theater company.

The next consideration for NJT is whether to develop a touring program that introduces its artistic work to audiences around the country, or to build upon its local base and found a school of performance arts that shares NJT's vision and mission with the community. The board, staff, and Black are looking into these possibilities, while also developing a succession plan to implement when Black decides to move on or retire.

Signs of Return to Stage Four

Sometimes while in Stage Five, organizations introduce a new element into their system. This often precipitates a return—in whole or in part—to an earlier stage of development. In this case, NJT recycles back to Stage Four—a life stage that focuses on growing internal systems, developing new products, and sustaining the organization. Some signs of this return are: a well-rounded director, refocus on the mission, the shoring up of many administrative systems (such as new office equipment), the addition of several operational staff members (such as a bookkeeper and administrative assistant), implementation of more comprehensive and strategic marketing, the development of a strategic plan, development of opportunities to expand programs and services, and the expansion of the board of directors. With these in place, NJT can expect to function well for many years—and eventually to renew itself again.

How to Know If You're Heading toward Decline and Dissolution

No matter what stage they're in, organizations can be well or ill. An unhealthy organization is alienated and isolated, often by lack of action or inappropriate action. The unhealthy organization lacks passion, experiences high levels of personalized conflict, or suffers from severe financial and programmatic crises. The more mature the organization, the greater the complexity and the more possibilities for things to go awry. If there are crises in a majority of the seven arenas, the organization is probably too far gone to recover. It will either dissolve gracefully—or painfully. For organizations in this situation the primary question should be, "Should we close?" If the crises do not pervade a majority of the arenas, dissolution *can* be averted by aggressive turnaround strategies.

The checklist that follows will help alert organizations to some areas of concern but does not specifically address an organization in distress. For this reason, signs of ill health in each of the seven arenas are listed below with a notation indicating which stage the signs more often occur. This list may be used as a checklist of red flags for the organization. The more signs checked, the more serious the organization's predicament and the more intervention needed.

Governance

- ❏ The organization's board generally rubber-stamps decisions without discussion or knowledge of the issues (Stages 3–5).
- ❏ Attendance at board meetings is consistently less than 50 percent (Stages 2–5).
- ❏ Only 20 to 30 percent of board attendees are the same from month to month (Stages 3–5).
- ❏ No new board members have joined the organizations in several years (Stages 3–5).
- ❏ More than 75 percent of the board has turned over in the last two years (Stages 3–5).
- ❏ There is ongoing, overt, and demoralizing conflict between board and staff (Stages 3–5).
- ❏ Board members cannot let go of their involvement in day-to-day operations (Stage 3).
- ❏ Board members are consistently and vehemently disagreeing and engaged in negative interactions with each other (Stages 3–5).
- ❏ Board members cannot agree on the primary mission of the organization (Stages 2–5).
- ❏ The board is unwilling/unable to replace an ineffective board chair (Stages 2–5).
- ❏ The board lacks skills in key areas like financial and legal expertise (Stages 3–5).
- ❏ Individual board members are bad-mouthing the organization outside of board meetings (Stages 3–5).

Staff leadership

- ❑ The executive director makes all decisions and rarely, if ever, consults with the board of directors before implementing the decisions (Stages 3–5).
- ❑ The executive director allows the board to make all the decisions (Stages 2–3).
- ❑ The executive director is in continual negative conflict with the board (Stages 3–5).

- ❑ The executive director is inaccessible—never returning phone calls and seemingly disengaged from the organization (Stages 2–5).
- ❑ The executive director is consistently unable to meet deadlines or tend to priority business (Stages 2–5).
- ❑ The executive director is the focus of a large number of complaints and grievances to the board (Stages 2–5).

Financing

- ❑ The organization is unable to meet payroll (Stages 2–5).
- ❑ The organization is consistently behind on payment of invoices (Stages 3–5).
- ❑ The organization's receivables are consistently more than ninety days old. (Stages 3–5).
- ❑ The organization fails or has significant warnings from an audit (Stages 3–5).

- ❑ The organization consistently relies on cash advances or a line of credit to balance its budget (Stages 3–5).
- ❑ More than 30 percent of the funds come from a single source (Stages 2–5).
- ❑ New directions in fundraising are always discussed but no actions are taken (Stages 4–5).
- ❑ A large number of funders are terminating or threatening to terminate agreements with the organization (Stages 4–5).

Administrative systems

- ❑ Critical administrative records such as tax forms, personnel policies, and client files cannot be retrieved (Stages 3–5).
- ❑ Legal compliance with human resource practices is in question (Stages 3–5).

- ❑ The organization's financial staff cannot provide an accurate financial picture (Stages 3–5).
- ❑ Well-developed systems are really bureaucratic nightmares (Stages 4–5).

Staffing

- ❑ There is high turnover of staff (Stages 3–5).
- ❑ Positions go unfilled for a year or longer (Stages 4–5).
- ❑ Staff morale is extremely low (Stages 3–5).
- ❑ Staff members bypass the executive director and take grievances directly to the board (Stages 2–3).
- ❑ Roles and responsibilities are unclear, causing confusion and negative conflict (Stages 3-5).

Products and services

- ❑ There is evidence that product and service quality has greatly declined (Stages 3–5).
- ❑ Referrals have dropped significantly (Stages 3–5).
- ❑ There is no process for evaluating products and services (Stages 3–4).
- ❑ Licensing or accreditation is in jeopardy (Stages 3–5).

Marketing

- ❑ There is no marketing strategy or current promotional materials in place (Stages 4–5).
- ❑ Key constituents cannot clearly define the purpose, products, or services of the organization (Stages 3–5).
- ❑ There is general perception and rumor that the organization is in crisis (Stages 3–5).
- ❑ The organization has received ongoing and substantial negative press (Stages 3–5).

Obstacles and opportunities

Obstacles

An agency on a steep path of decline may have too many obstacles to overcome. To the extent that inappropriate leadership, financial crises, legal proceedings against the agency, and a general lack of passion are all working together these will pull the agency to its end.

Opportunities

The bright side of knowing that you are on a path of decline is the hope for significant turnaround in the problem areas, or in the case of too many problem areas, a graceful dissolution and the chance to move on to new endeavors. Putting closure to the conflicts and the struggles is a positive force in extremely dysfunctional organizations.

Tips for moving through decline

Overall Question	*Should we close?*
Overall Approach	*Take the time to engage an external, unbiased party to help the organization through this time of crisis. Look carefully at each arena of the organization and then at all the arenas together. After comprehensive analysis determine whether the organization is salvageable, should be merged with another organization, or should be dissolved. Below are turnaround strategies to address problems in each of the arenas. If the organization decides to merge or dissolve, legal counsel should be sought.*
Governance	• Hold a board meeting to ensure that all board members are well-informed and in agreement on action steps. • Engage a third party to mediate disputes or disagreements.[7] • Have the board resign or build the board anew.
Staff Leadership	• Hire a coach to work with the executive director on specific areas of weakness.
Financing	• Engage an external consultant to review finances, make recommendations and implement improvements. • Meet with funders to explain the financial situation. • Develop a short-term plan for addressing financial difficulties.
Administrative Systems	• Shore up systems that aren't working.
Staffing	• Engage a third party to mediate disputes or disagreements. • Schedule a staff retreat to address the critical staff issues. • Develop a long-term plan to address staff burn out.
Products and Services	• Take immediate action to ensure quality of service—this may mean shutting down certain activities.
Marketing	• Engage technical assistance in crisis communication management.

---

[7] For guidance on selecting mediation specialists, see Angelica (1999).

Some Closing Thoughts

As you read the detailed description of each stage, you were likely able to identify several factors occurring in your own organization. If it all seems overwhelming or if you need a quick reference, Table 6 on page 44 summarizes the primary questions, obstacles, and opportunities of each stage.

At this point, you probably have a fair idea where your organization fits into this model; the assessment tool in chapter two will help you refine the picture. But remember: this model is ONLY a model. Your own perspective, or that of a trusted adviser, is most valuable.

Nonprofit organization growth, for most organizations, does develop in a patterned way. Stages of more mature development follow those of less mature development in a remarkably predictable manner. To a large (but general) extent, we can forecast organizational behaviors based on what we observe of the organization in the present.

Life cycle norms are only *averages*. Your nonprofit organization may be ahead of or behind these averages. So, if a certain behavior is characteristic of a Stage Four organization, and your ten-year-old-organization has not reached this stage yet, you should not feel that you have cause to worry. Your nonprofit organization may be a little slower than the average. Likewise, if your two-year-old organization excels in a particular arena, you may still be primarily in an early stage of development. Every nonprofit organization has its own timetable.

And then, of course, there are individual differences. An organization may have most of the characteristics of Stage Two *and* be building good policies and procedures (Stage Three work). A Stage Four organization may be running flawlessly but still be wrestling with ongoing finance problems more typical of a younger organization.

The knowledge of life cycle stages should not be a reason for worry—quite the opposite. Since the model is an average, it is normal for organizations to deviate from it. "Now I know we're normal" is what many nonprofit employees and board members say when they read the descriptions of different stages. It is hoped the model will prepare you to feel comfortable with your nonprofit organization's experiences as it ages and give you the confidence to act with authority as the organization changes.

◆　　◆　　◆

Up to this point we have looked at the overall life cycle concept and the stages themselves in detail. The next chapter presents a Life Stage Assessment Tool. This tool is designed to help organizations determine what life stage they are in and think about the relative strengths and weaknesses of their organization given its life cycle stage.

> "Now I know we're normal" is what many nonprofit employees and board members say when they read the descriptions of different stages.

Table 6. Obstacles and Opportunities of Nonprofit Organization Life Cycle Stages

Stage	Primary Question	Obstacles	Opportunities
1: Imagine and Inspire	Can this dream be realized?	• Resistance to formalizing • Lack of funding • Lack of expertise • No outside support	• Creativity and energy of the dream • New people latching onto the dream
2: Found and Frame	How are we going to pull this off?	• Fear of formalizing • Sustaining enthusiasm among supporters • Founders' energy difficult to corral	• Excitement of funders • People wanting to join the organization • Charismatic leader
3: Ground and Grow	How can we build this to be viable?	• Absence of systems of accountability • Overwhelmed with new elements entering the organizational system • Danger in remaining an isolated system • Chaos may alienate funders, clients, and staff	• Sense of accomplishment • New faces and voices • Diversification of the agency • Rejuvenating founders
4: Produce and Sustain	How can the momentum be sustained?	• Lack of control or too much control • Lack of risk taking • Board unable to move to a governing role • Too much focus on day-to-day operations • Conflict between old and new	• Feeling of security • Adequate human and financial resources • New staff and board brings fresh ideas • Ability to take risks
5: Review and Renew	What do we need to redesign?	• Resistance to change • Isolation of the agency • Inability to address internal or external changes	• Wisdom from the past • Energized and committed staff • Opportunities for new partners and allies
Signs of Decline and Dissolution	Should we close?	• Financial crisis • Inappropriate leadership • Inability to change • Lack of passion	• Hope for a graceful ending, merger, or spin-off • Commitment to a significant turn-around

Chapter Two

Nonprofit Life Stage Assessment

THIS BOOK OUTLINES A PATH of development for a typical nonprofit organization, based on patterns and similarities shared by many nonprofit organizations. The *Nonprofit Life Stage Assessment* is a tool for determining what life stage an organization is in. It helps you understand your organization's strengths and weaknesses with respect to its particular stage of development. The tool will help your organization plan for future needs, make decisions proactively, anticipate challenges, and determine what adjustments might be appropriate. Additionally, knowledge about your organization's stage of development will help you realize that some of the challenges your organization is experiencing are normal.

The authors designed this tool with these purposes in mind:

- To provide insights on the stages of development of nonprofit organizations.
- As a tool for executive directors, boards of directors, and consultants who want to help nonprofit organizations grow and develop.
- As a discussion tool between boards of directors and employees.
- To provide benchmarks against which nonprofit organizations can gauge themselves.

You can use the results of the assessment on several different levels. On one level, your responses to the assessment tool will place your organization in a "home stage" that shows your overall location within the model. On another level, it shows your organization's strengths and weaknesses relative to its home stage. On a third level it can be used to compare your organization against generally recognized practices for high-functioning nonprofit organizations.

Organizations may find the tool especially helpful in the following situations:

- Prior to embarking on a strategic planning process
- During times of high stress or challenge for the organization
- When engaging an organization development consultant
- Prior to an executive search
- As preparation for discussion at a board or staff retreat

There are three ways to administer the assessment:

1. It can be used with an individual in a leadership role in the organization such as the executive director or board chair, and the results can be discussed with a knowledgeable third party such as an organizational consultant.

2. Copies can be distributed to a number of members of the organization, and the results can be collated and presented to interested parties such as the board of directors or key staff.

3. The tool can also be administered in a group session, with a collective score for each statement.

You can also take the Nonprofit Life Stage Assessment online at the publisher's web site. Visit www.FieldstoneAlliance.org and search for the Nonprofit Life Stage Assessment.

The Nonprofit Life Stage Assessment

Instructions

On a scale of 1 to 5 (1 = Least Like Us, 5 = Most Like Us), enter the number that best represents the current state of your organization in the box to the right of each question. After every three questions, add up your responses for those three questions and enter the sum in the Group Total box that follows. Be sure to answer all questions. We recognize there is repetition of some concepts, however, the individual questions are phrased slightly differently. This repetition is important to determining the developmental stage of the organization. We do not recommend answering selective statements within an arena or stage, as the results will be skewed.

After entering all group totals within an arena, compare them to determine which is highest. Enter the label for the highest group total at the bottom of the page. If there are one or more other group totals that are within two points of the highest group total, also enter their labels at the bottom of the page.

The assessment should take 20 to 30 minutes to complete.

Here's an example:

		Least like us			Most like us	
		1	2	3	4	5

A. Governance

		Score
A1	1. We are in the process of writing our first set of articles of incorporation or bylaws for our new organization.	1
	2. We do not yet have an "official, duly elected" board of directors.	1
	3. We do not have our first *written* strategic plan with measurable objectives and action steps for the organization.	1
	Total A1	**3**
A2	4. Our organization has adopted its first set of articles of incorporation and bylaws.	3
	5. Most, if not all, of the current board members knew each other before joining the board and many agreed to serve on the board because they were personal friends of the founder or founders.	3
	6. Our board sees itself as more of a "hands-on working board" rather than a "hands-off policy board."	3
	Total A2	**9**
A3	7. The board of directors is about evenly split between those who joined the board at the personal request of the founders of the organization and those who joined after the board began a formal recruitment and nominating process for new board members.	1
	8. The organization recruits board members as much for their expertise and experience as for their passion for the organization's work.	3
	9. The organization is still primarily *reacting* to external forces more than planning how the organization will take advantage of external forces "on the horizon."	2
	Total A3	**6**
A4	10. Our organization needs to complete or has recently completed its first comprehensive strategic planning process.	2
	11. The current composition of the board makes it easier than before to raise questions about our purpose and mission, establish written governance policies, and begin to set a strategic direction.	4
	12. The executive director and the board have a pretty clear sense of the division of roles and responsibilities for the governance and daily operation of the organization.	1
	Total A4	**7**
A5	13. Our organization has conducted several formal strategic planning processes since the founding of the organization.	4
	14. The executive director and the board of directors have a written document that describes the division of roles and responsibilities for the governance and daily operations of the organization.	3
	15. Our organization could use a sense of renewal, re-energizing, and refocusing.	4
	Total A5	**11**
	Highest group total	**A5**
	Group totals within one point of highest, if any	**None**

The Nonprofit Life Stage Assessment

		Least like us			Most like us	
		1	2	3	4	5

A. Governance

A1	1. We are in the process of writing our first set of articles of incorporation or bylaws for our new organization.	
	2. We do not yet have an "official, duly elected" board of directors.	
	3. We do not have our first *written* strategic plan with measurable objectives and action steps for the organization.	
	Total A1	
A2	4. Our organization has adopted its first set of articles of incorporation and bylaws.	
	5. Most, if not all, of the current board members knew each other before joining the board and many agreed to serve on the board because they were personal friends of the founder or founders.	
	6. Our board sees itself as more of a "hands-on working board" rather than a "hands-off policy board."	
	Total A2	
A3	7. The board of directors is about evenly split between those who joined the board at the personal request of the founders of the organization and those who joined after the board began a formal recruitment and nominating process for new board members.	
	8. The organization recruits board members as much for their expertise and experience as for their passion for the organization's work.	
	9. The organization is still primarily *reacting* to external forces more than planning how the organization will take advantage of external forces "on the horizon."	
	Total A3	
A4	10. Our organization needs to complete or has recently completed its first comprehensive strategic planning process.	
	11. The current composition of the board makes it easier than before to raise questions about our purpose and mission, establish written governance policies, and begin to set a strategic direction.	
	12. The executive director and the board have a pretty clear sense of the division of roles and responsibilities for the governance and daily operation of the organization.	
	Total A4	
A5	13. Our organization has conducted several formal strategic planning processes since the founding of the organization.	
	14. The executive director and the board of directors have a written document that describes the division of roles and responsibilities for the governance and daily operations of the organization.	
	15. Our organization could use a sense of renewal, re-energizing, and refocusing.	
	Total A5	
	Highest group total	
	Group totals within one point of highest, if any	

		Least like us			Most like us	
		1	2	3	4	5
B. Staff Leadership						
B1	1. We are not seeing a need at this time for a paid executive director.					
	2. Board members tend to be the contact persons for the organization.					
	3. The vision and concept for the organization resides more in the minds of the founders than anywhere else.					
	Total B1					
B2	4. Our leader is more visionary and entrepreneurial than operational.					
	5. Our leader makes all the decisions for the organization.					
	6. Our leader prefers to act with minimal participation from the board, staff, or volunteers.					
	Total B2					
B3	7. The organization has a full-time paid executive director.					
	8. The executive director makes most but not all the decisions and involves the staff and board in some of the decisions.					
	9. The organization needs the executive director to begin separating their time between the daily operations of the organization and meeting with potential funders, community leaders, and other nonprofit executive directors.					
	Total B3					
B4	10. Our executive director is ready and able to lead the organization in expanding its mission and program offerings to meet the needs of the community.					
	11. The addition of program managers strengthens the organization and has not hindered timely decision making or staff flexibility.					
	12. The executive director consciously divides her or his time between tending to the internal operations of the organization and the external relationships with the community, funders, and other executive directors.					
	Total B4					
B5	13. Our organization has an executive director who is decisive and able to work collaboratively.					
	14. Our organization has an executive director who understands non-profit finances and organizational development concepts.					
	15. Our organization's founder is long gone from the organization.					
	Total B5					
	Highest group total					
	Group totals within one point of highest, if any					

		Least like us			Most like us	
		1	2	3	4	5
C. Financing						
C1	1. Our revenue is primarily donations from individuals. Little if any of the revenue is derived from foundations or corporations or contracts with other nonprofit or public sector organizations.					
	2. We are discussing the feasibility of writing grants or negotiating contracts for additional revenue.					
	3. We need to write our first one-year budget. Revenue and expenses are based more on projections than historical financial data.					
	Total C1					
C2	4. Our organization has yet to develop a written plan for financing the work of the organization.					
	5. Our organization's current sources of funding are sufficient for the work we are doing.					
	6. Our organization is in the process of preparing its first grant application for operational support.					
	Total C2					
C3	7. Our organization has a fundraising plan, not necessarily written, which generally targets specific funding sources rather than using a "shotgun" approach to fundraising.					
	8. Our organization can produce all the financial documents that could be required by a funding source (for example multi-year budget, balance sheet, audit, cash flow analysis).					
	9. The executive director, staff, and volunteers are discussing additional services and programs which would produce more revenue for the organization.					
	Total C3					
C4	10. Our organization has funding which is a combination of income sources, namely earned income, donated income, contracted income, and investment income rather than being dependent on one or two sources of income.					
	11. Our organization has a steady cash flow, adequate accounting systems, and an operational budget.					
	12. As an organization, we are exploring new and expanded revenue sources to supplement our core funding. We have or are about to hire or contract fundraising staff.					
	Total C4					
C5	13. Our organization needs to develop and sustain new financing sources.					
	14. Our organization needs to diversify its funding base to include several different sources of funds, such as public, private, fees, contracts, donations, foundations, and endowments.					
	15. Our organization has established or is planning to establish investment policies, planned giving, and endowments.					
	Total C5					
	Highest group total					
	Group totals within one point of highest, if any					

		Least like us			Most like us	
		1	2	3	4	5
D. Administrative Systems						
D1	1. There is not a need for office space at this point in time.					
	2. There is not a need for the organization to have a written policy and procedure manual at this point in time.					
	3. Setting up payroll, accounting, and human resources functions are the least of our concerns at this time.					
	Total D1					
D2	4. Administrative duties are the responsibility of board members, volunteers, and any paid staff.					
	5. Our organization tends to follow mostly what is written in state and federal law because we have not written our own policy and procedure manual.					
	6. Our organization uses a volunteer or fiscal agent to manage all of our finances.					
	Total D2					
D3	7. Our organization will gain greater credibility and stability with our own office space.					
	8. Our organization has hired a staff person (or plans to hire a staff person) whose primary duty is to manage the office.					
	9. Our organization has grown large enough that it is time to hire a business manager and manage our own finances rather than pay a fiscal agent.					
	Total D3					
D4	10. The organization has an automated record system that keeps track of people using our services.					
	11. Our organization is considering expansion of leased space or purchase of office space.					
	12. The organization has and generally uses personnel policies, salary schedules, annual performance reviews, and formal job descriptions.					
	Total D4					
D5	13. It is time to begin revamping and updating our administrative systems.					
	14. The organization has departments and those departments can make administrative decisions that fall within the approved policies and procedures of the organization.					
	15. Our organization is experiencing tension about the degree of centralization or decentralization needed in the organization.					
	Total D5					
	Highest group total					
	Group totals within one point of highest, if any					

		Least like us			Most like us	
		1	2	3	4	5
E. Staffing						
E1	1. We have few if any written job descriptions.					
	2. The organization has no paid staff. Volunteers do all the work of the organization.					
	3. The organization does not have clearly identified supervisory and reporting relationships among the volunteers.					
	Total E1					
E2	4. Our organization is run predominantly by volunteers, but we still have paid part-time staff.					
	5. Our organization is thinking about what we will eventually need in order for paid and unpaid staff to run our programs.					
	6. Our organization generally relies on in-kind donations of specialized advice, such as legal, program, or financial.					
	Total E2					
E3	7. Our organization has approximately an equal number of volunteers and paid staff doing the work of the organization.					
	8. As an organization, we believe that too many policies and procedures will interfere with meeting community needs.					
	9. Our organization is finding a greater need for staff with skills specific to our program needs rather than just generalists or all-purpose staff.					
	Total E3					
E4	10. Our organization's staff is growing more specialized in its functions and expertise and this is a positive development.					
	11. Our organization's management and staff tend to operate using cross-functional, results-oriented work teams that make most of the decisions affecting their work.					
	12. Our organization is experiencing a mix of old and new staff plus a diversity of staff including race, culture, gender, age, and graduate degrees.					
	Total E4					
E5	13. Our organization is going through a period of high staff turnover and low employee morale.					
	14. Our organization has found a comfortable balance between providing service exclusively and providing service through joint or collaborative ventures.					
	15. Our organization has high-performing, interdependent, and self-sufficient work teams.					
	Total E5					
	Highest group total					
	Group totals within one point of highest, if any					

		Least like us			Most like us	
		1	2	3	4	5
F. Products and Services						
F1	1. We still are not sure what products or services our organization would offer on an ongoing basis.					
	2. We are in the process of assessing the community needs relative to the mission of our organization.					
	3. We are generating lots of ideas for what kind of products and services we could or should provide.					
	Total F1					
F2	4. Our organization is moving from talking about products and services to actually offering them.					
	5. Although the organization has plans and ideas for more products and services, our resources limit us to smaller activities for the moment.					
	6. Our organization thinks our products and services will do well and meet a need, but we lack the evaluation systems to know if we are doing well.					
	Total F2					
F3	7. Our organization has to make decisions about whether or not to develop activities that have a high potential for funding but are not entirely consistent with the mission of the organization.					
	8. We would like to add additional products and services but lack the staff and space to do so.					
	9. Our organization is refining and improving our current products and services before adding new ones.					
	Total F3					
F4	10. The organization's products and services are well designed and operated.					
	11. The organization's success and visibility has led to opportunities to branch off in a variety of directions.					
	12. The organization has a routine, formal evaluation process for all its programs and activities. The organization will use the information to enhance, maintain, or end programs within the organization.					
	Total F4					
F5	13. Our organization has a schedule for conducting evaluation of products and services.					
	14. Our organization has 30 to 60 percent joint programs with other nonprofit or for-profit organizations.					
	15. Our organization's products and services need to be redesigned to meet emerging client needs.					
	Total F5					
	Highest group total					
	Group totals within one point of highest, if any					

		Least like us			Most like us	
		1	2	3	4	5
G. Marketing						
G1	1. Very few people or organizations know we exist.					
	2. We are still debating who or what is the market for our services.					
	3. Although we think about it, a brochure is a future action item.					
	Total G1					
G2	4. We market ourselves primarily by word of mouth.					
	5. We are too busy with other organizational responsibilities to put time toward a marketing campaign.					
	6. We print our brochures, announcements, handouts, and other marketing materials using forms and examples found in our computer programs. We are not paying a consultant to produce brochures, announcements, or handouts.					
	Total G2					
G3	7. Our promotional goals are adequately met with a simple black-and-white fact sheet or brochure.					
	8. While we would like a comprehensive marketing campaign (brochures, flyers, annual reports, web site, advertising), we don't have the funds to pay for it.					
	9. We need to refine our image and identify our target audiences for our services.					
	Total G3					
G4	10. The organization's marketing materials have a consistent design and convey consistent key messages to promote instant recognition.					
	11. Our organization routinely produces and distributes annual reports and newsletters.					
	12. The organization needs a marketing plan to publicize its products and services.					
	Total G4					
G5	13. Our organization's message and marketing plan are not in tune with today's market and the needs of people.					
	14. Our marketing approach must change to reflect our changed mission or programming niche.					
	15. Our organization has the necessary resources—such as money, staff time, volunteers, experience—to support changes in the marketing plan.					
	Total G5					
	Highest group total					
	Group totals within one point of highest, if any					

Plotting and Understanding Your Score

1. Shade in the box for the highest group total in each arena below. For example, if your highest score in Governance was "A5," shade the box labeled "A5."

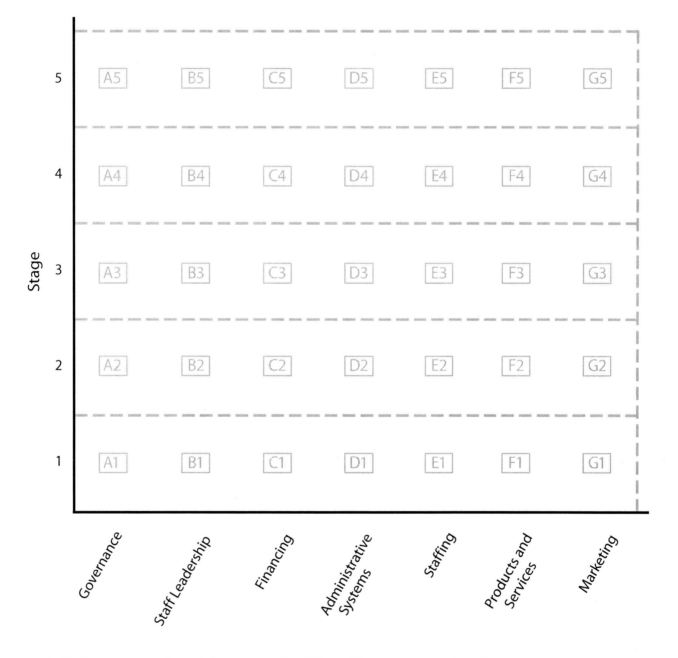

2. Review the score sheet. A home stage should be evident as you see where the shaded boxes fall horizontally across the chart. But if you want to confirm your own intuition or pinpoint your home stage more precisely, go to the next step.

3. Return to the arena questions.

   a) Insert the total for each set of arena questions on the chart below. You will find that the questions are organized into clusters of three. Each cluster corresponds to a stage. You will be entering thirty-five numbers.

   b) Total the numbers in each column. The column with the highest total score is your organization's home stage. This shows your organization's current stage of development. The stage with the second highest score is your organization's next preferred operating stage.

ARENA	STAGE 1 Imagine and Inspire		STAGE 2 Found and Frame		STAGE 3 Ground and Grow		STAGE 4 Produce and Sustain		STAGE 5 Review and Renew	
Governance	A1		A2		A3		A4		A5	
Staff Leadership	B1		B2		B3		B4		B5	
Financing	C1		C2		C3		C4		C5	
Administrative Systems	D1		D2		D3		D4		D5	
Staffing	E1		E2		E3		E4		E5	
Products and Services	F1		F2		F3		F4		F5	
Marketing	G1		G2		G3		G4		G5	
TOTALS:										

   c) On the score sheet on the previous page, draw a horizontal box around all the arena boxes of your home stage. This allows you to compare your status in each arena (governance, staffing, and so forth) with your home stage. You can see which arenas may need some improvement (those below your home stage), and in which arenas you are moving ahead (those above). This may guide your thinking about strategies to help the organization progress to its most functional state.

Here's an example: An established community development corporation took the inventory and came up with a high score in Stage Four, as shown below.

ARENA	STAGE 1 Imagine and Inspire		STAGE 2 Found and Frame		STAGE 3 Ground and Grow		STAGE 4 Produce and Sustain		STAGE 5 Review and Renew	
Governance	A1	3	A2	9	A3	6	A4	7	A5	11
Staff Leadership	B1	3	B2	5	B3	11	B4	15	B5	15
Financing	C1	3	C2	5	C3	13	C4	15	C5	11
Administrative Systems	D1	9	D2	3	D3	7	D4	11	D5	7
Staffing	E1	3	E2	3	E3	6	E4	13	E5	10
Products and Services	F1	7	F2	3	F3	5	F4	15	F5	11
Marketing	G1	3	G2	3	G3	3	G4	9	G5	7
TOTALS:		31		31		51		85		72

The organization then traced its home stage across the score sheet, as shown below.

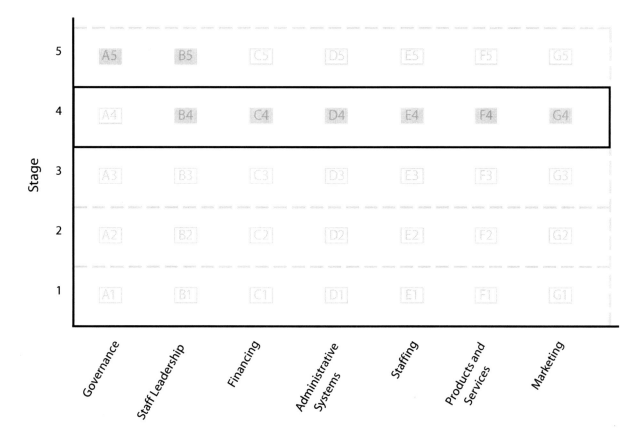

As you can see, while most of the organization's high arena scores are in Stage Four, governance is in Stage Five, and the organization has equal arena scores for staff leadership in Stages Four and Five. It's not unusual for an organization to be moving ahead in some arenas or lagging behind in others. You can use this awareness of your variance from the home stage to plan for changes in the organization.

Explore the Results

Review your score sheet and your chart in section 3b on page 56. Check for arena scores that are high or low. In the previous example, the organization could explore reasons why Governance has clearly moved into Stage Five, while Staff Leadership is on the cusp of Four and Five.

For deeper discussion, check your responses to specific questions. For example, your organization may have a home stage of Four, but has ranked question 1 in the Staffing arena with only a score of 1 (least like us) and question 3 in the Products and Services arena with a score of just 2. This could indicate specific areas of weakness that might need attention.

If you have any concerns about the overall health of your organization, review the elements of organizations in distress described on pages 39–41 and check your organization against them.

While you will have a home stage that represents the current functioning level of your organization, your organization will also have elements of all four other stages. As mentioned in the beginning of this book, it is possible that your organization as a whole might generally be in one home stage, but certain programs or arenas might be in a different stage. As your home stage progresses from Stage One to Five over time, you must acknowledge and pass through the previous developmental stages. The knowledge, experience, and information gained at each stage are needed in order to progress to the next stage.

At this point you may be asking the most basic question: "We're in Stage Four—*so what*?" The life stages model and this assessment tool are *not* science. They are just a useful construct to help you think about your organization. With that in mind, consider the following questions to help you explore the meaning of the results for your organization. These questions could be answered by the executive director or board chair or as part of a group discussion.

1. Overall, do you agree with the results—does the home stage identified by the assessment tool match your perception of your organization? Why or why not?

2. The model does seem to fit a number of nonprofit organizations. If your organization *does not* match the tool or the model, why? What are some of the unique attributes of your organization that differentiate it from other nonprofit organizations? How can you capitalize on those attributes? What benefits and risks might accompany those differences?

3. What are the key issues or struggles for your organization at this stage?

4. What strengths does your organization draw from this stage?

5. What do you want to leave behind from the previous stage? What do you want to carry forward from the previous stage?

6. To move to the next stage, what are the arenas needing improvement and attention? What actions might you take to minimize the obstacles and maximize the opportunities you face?

7. If your organization is in or nearing Stage Five, what arenas need attention to sustain your organization?

8. What do you need to learn to be successful in your life cycle journey? Where or to whom can you go to get this information?

Organizations with unusual results

Equally high scores in two adjacent stages

Sometimes organizations find that they have equally high (or nearly equal) scores in two stages. Usually those stages are adjacent (for example, nearly identical scores for Stages Three and Four). Here's an example of such an organization:

ARENA	STAGE 1 Imagine and Inspire		STAGE 2 Found and Frame		STAGE 3 Ground and Grow		STAGE 4 Produce and Sustain		STAGE 5 Review and Renew	
Governance	A1	4	A2	5	A3	8	A4	5	A5	12
Staff Leadership	B1	3	B2	8	B3	11	B4	12	B5	12
Financing	C1	7	C2	5	C3	14	C4	8	C5	11
Administrative Systems	D1	3	D2	5	D3	4	D4	11	D5	6
Staffing	E1	3	E2	6	E3	7	E4	9	E5	10
Products and Services	F1	7	F2	7	F3	9	F4	11	F5	9
Marketing	G1	6	G2	6	G3	9	G4	12	G5	8
TOTALS:	33		42		62		68		68	

If this is the case, our experience with using this model suggests that your organization is in a transition from one stage to the next. You have elements of both stages, without a clear home stage. If you were to score your organization again in a year, it is likely that it would have a distinct home stage.

Equally high scores in two nonadjacent stages

If you have nearly equal high scores in two or more stages that are *not* adjacent (for example, Stages Three and Five), it is possible that the model doesn't apply well to your organization, or that the questions in the tool do not successfully differentiate what is occurring in your organization. Here is an example of such an organization:

ARENA	STAGE 1 Imagine and Inspire		STAGE 2 Found and Frame		STAGE 3 Ground and Grow		STAGE 4 Produce and Sustain		STAGE 5 Review and Renew	
Governance	A1	3	A2	4	A3	9	A4	6	A5	13
Staff Leadership	B1	3	B2	7	B3	9	B4	10	B5	15
Financing	C1	3	C2	5	C3	15	C4	8	C5	11
Administrative Systems	D1	3	D2	3	D3	11	D4	6	D5	5
Staffing	E1	3	E2	3	E3	5	E4	7	E5	8
Products and Services	F1	9	F2	7	F3	9	F4	8	F5	10
Marketing	G1	3	G2	6	G3	11	G4	6	G5	7
TOTALS:		27		35		69		51		69

If this is the case for your organization, you can still review your responses to the individual questions, the description of the stages, and the discussion questions above to help you think about actions you might take to ensure your organization's success. Use the assessment tool to spur thought and discussion, even if the tool or model doesn't fit your organization.

High arena scores that are two or more stages apart from your home stage

High arena scores that are two or more stages apart from your home stage may indicate either a lack of expertise or extraordinary expertise in those arenas. Here's an example of one such organization.

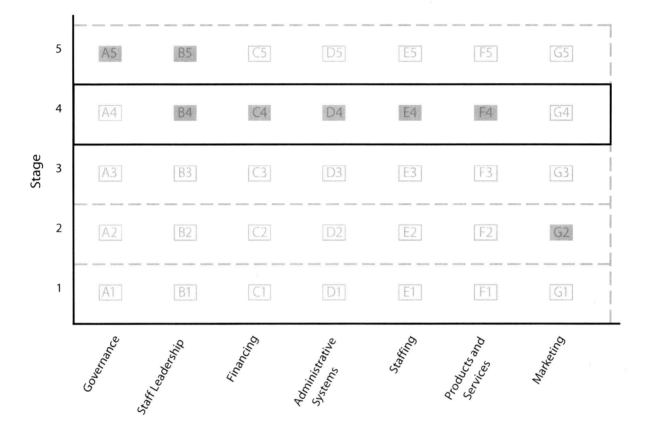

This organization's home stage is Four, but it's still at Stage Two in marketing. This organization may not have adequate expertise in marketing for its developmental stage. Use the assessment tool to help guide your discussion on discrepant scores like these for your organization.

No apparent home stage or great variety in arena scores for each stage

Sometimes the scores are all over the map. Here's an example:

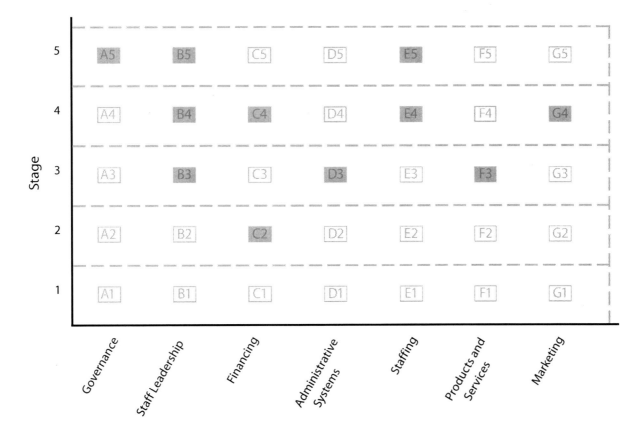

Lack of clarity or great variety among arena scores may be due to a number of factors. As noted earlier, sometimes the model just doesn't apply. It may be that your organization is experiencing ambiguity or turmoil, and this shows up as a wide variation in the scoring. It is also possible that the people taking the inventory have very different views of the organization, skewing the results. Regardless of the reason, explore the results and responses to better understand your organization's current status.

Summary

This chapter has helped you assess your organization's life stage. The next chapter includes descriptions and analyses of organizations at each of the life stages and offers suggestions that each organization might consider as it develops.

Chapter Three

Examples, Analysis, and Advice

NOW THAT YOU HAVE A DESCRIPTION of each stage and a sense about which stage your organization is in, it's time to figure out how to make the most of that stage or what steps to take that will move you to the next stage. As said previously, every organization is unique, so it is difficult to prescribe exactly what actions must be taken in a particular stage. What follows is an example of an organization in each of the life stages.[8] Each example presents a scenario, an analysis of the situation, and advice about what action steps that particular organization could take.

Conflicts R Us: *An Organization in Stage One*

Conflicts R Us is well on its way to forming two highly successful nonprofit entities in the northern and southern parts of the country of Cyprus. It all started when an American was asked to come to Cyprus to train Cypriots in mediation skills. After a year-long mediation skills training program for more than two hundred Cyprus citizens from all walks of life, the participants and the trainer asked, "Now what?" The trainer envisioned establishing an organization in Cyprus that would use these trained mediators to resolve a variety of conflicts. Using a mediation center model from the United States, the trainer began to talk with some of the trainees about his vision. Two trainees became particularly interested and saw great value in establishing a mediation center in Cyprus. The United Nations, which had funded the initial training, also seemed intrigued by the idea and offered to fund the establishment of such a center. After the American trainer returned to the United States the two interested trainees then became the stewards of the vision. They talked to many others about the idea.

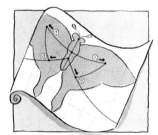

Imagine and Inspire

---

8 These case studies are based on real organizations, but details have been changed to preserve confidentiality.

Currently they are in discussion with two potential funders, several government officials, and other alumni of the training. They hope to develop a proposal in the next few months and open Cyprus' first mediation center by the end of the year.

Analysis

This group, which is not yet an incorporated organization, is clearly in Stage One. There is a vision, a dream, and a sense that by creating an organization the vision can be realized. While the "founder" is no longer involved (an unusual scenario for a Stage One organization), the vision has been passed on to two other individuals. These individuals are as impassioned by the idea as the founder and have begun to get others enthused as well. The energy and enthusiasm about the manifestation of the idea is a critical aspect of Stage One.

Moving from a dream to reality will require money and more than two people.

Advice

The two "champions" of the vision need to continue to garner support. If they are to move effectively from Stage One to Stage Two they will need to write a concept paper, business plan, or both. Articulating on paper the purpose, benefit, and costs of a mediation center will enable others to say whether or not they can commit to it. The two champions must also court important supporters. Moving from dream to reality will require money and the efforts of more than two people. To move to the next steps in creating the organization, the now-founders need to target one or more sources for start-up money and find someone who can devote the time to getting the organization off the ground.

There are several steps that can be taken to ready the organization for its next stage:

- Locate helpful resources—the Internet, books, people, other organizations with shared values and helpful experience. Look for advice and assistance in deciding whether to incorporate and how to do so.

- Make the vision explicit—usually through the creation of a concept paper and business plan. State the mission, goals, structure, and costs involved in bringing the organization to life.

- Contact local management assistance programs to determine how to incorporate as a nonprofit.

- Begin cultivating prospective donors. If the dream becomes reality, funding will be needed. Start now to build interest and enthusiasm among potential funders; early relationships with potential donors can have long-term benefits.

Free Again: *An Organization in Stage Two*

Free Again is a three-year-old preschool with a focus on multiculturalism and non-violence. It began as the dream of a group of people who had a vision for how children could be taught to be nonviolent using the gifts and talents of their cultural heritage. The founders located a dynamic woman to document the concept of the school and present it to a local commission studying school reform. The woman was known throughout the state as an activist in the early childhood arena. Intrigued by the concept paper, the local school district decided to make the preschool a special project. The school district then hired the woman to coordinate the project. The district provided space and start-up funding. In its first year, the coordinator developed a long list of goals for the project. She also convinced many people that the project was worth pursuing. She personally enticed some very influential people to join an advisory board for the school.

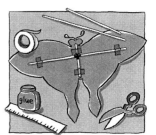

Found and Frame

After two years the school district and the advisory board jointly decided that the project should spin off and become a separate nonprofit agency. About six months later the initial coordinator moved out of state and a new coordinator was hired. Shortly after being hired, this new coordinator was named the executive director and the organization obtained its 501(c)(3) nonprofit status. The incorporation papers identified the advisory board as the organization's board of directors. The school district agreed to fund the agency, serve as its fiscal agent, and offer rent-free office space to the organization through its first year as a separate entity. Besides the executive director, there is a full time administrative support staff and a child development curriculum specialist.

The activities of the organization are accomplished through a broad network of volunteers. While expert consultants are hired when needed, the bulk of the work of the organization is accomplished through donations of time and energy. The executive director is excited about the innumerable possibilities for programs and activities but realizes there are a number of challenges ahead. Top on the list is finding appropriate board members who are willing to get more involved in the agency's development, planning ahead for self-sufficiency in financing, and deciding which services to really focus on.

Analysis

Free Again is clearly a Stage Two organization. It has taken the energy and enthusiasm displayed early on by the founders and created a stand-alone organization with its own 501(c)(3) status. By successfully garnering the resources (both in terms of people and funding) the organization proved that it was ready to be its own entity. Other indicators that the organization is in Stage Two is the retitling and appointment of the project coordinator to "executive director" and the retitling of the advisory board to "board of directors." Stage Two organizations commonly give people who have been part of the "founding" group positional titles in the newly formed organization. Also characteristic of Stage Two organizations is some form of start-up assistance such as a large grant or the use of donated office space, in this case, the school district. Other indications that the organization is in early stages of development are the broad network of volunteers, the low number of paid staff, the absence of long-term funding, and the lack of a process for making decisions about which program ideas to pursue.

Advice

The executive director is faced with a very exciting yet demanding task: sustain the enthusiasm for the mission and goals but address some very concrete issues like sustainable funding. The executive director must capitalize on the energy of the founders yet find a way to build the organization's identity beyond them. The need to develop administrative systems, raise additional funds, and recruit and train an effective board of directors may feel to the executive director and the board like a diversion from the "real work" of the organization. Yet addressing them is critical to the organization's survival. Following are several things the new organization can do to successfully navigate Stage Two.[9]

- Develop a fundraising plan. Work with someone who has been through an agency start-up to determine basic costs for the first two to three years. Develop a plan for how the funds will be raised and begin knocking on doors. These early funding relationships will pave the way for fundraising in later years of the organization's life.

- Create a strong board. Assess the key skills, talents, and passions needed on the board to get the organization through its first few years. Recruit new people to the organization—people who haven't been involved in the formation of the idea. Train the board on basic board roles and responsibilities so they know from the outset what their job is.

- Institute basic administrative systems such as standard accounting practices and procedures and record-keeping systems. Make sure the organization gets off on the right foot. It is easy for organizations in this stage to get so enthused by the programs and services that they forget about establishing some of the underpinning organizational practices that will enable them to succeed.

- Find a guide. All organizations have been through start-up. There is no need to reinvent the wheel or feel stuck. Find someone who has been through it and can provide advice and assistance as this new organization gets underway.

---

[9] For guidance on nonprofit start-up, see Hummel (1996) and Mancuso (1997).

Pets for People: *An Organization in Stage Three*

Pets for People is a four-year-old organization whose mission is to match animals with people who need their services. The program was started by the current executive director who, having found that his dog helped him cope with a painful loss, decided he wanted to develop a nonprofit that would provide animal companionship to people in need. He began the work in his home, gathering a handful of interested people to be the first board of directors and seeking funds to get his vision off the ground. The first board included his sister, a past business colleague, and a staff person at a local animal shelter—all close associates of the founder. He formed a 501(c)(3) organization and secured a $5,000 start-up grant to move the nonprofit from his home office to rented space. The modest board of three began to meet regularly. The organization selected its first demonstration dog and began serving its first clients within the first two years.

Ground and Grow

Over the next two years the program, finances, and board expanded. The organization received several awards for its work pairing dogs with disabled people. With the help of an agency that specialized in recruiting and placing board members, the board grew from the hand-picked three to ten members; the executive director's sister resigned in the process. There is a growing waiting list of clients and the executive director, although now receiving a pay check, has not taken a vacation since the organization's inception. Board meetings are consumed with reports of the wonderful work of the organization, but at each meeting the board is pressuring the executive director to develop better administrative systems. At a recent meeting the board strongly encouraged the executive director to produce cash flow statements and hire a full-time receptionist. The executive director is resisting taking action on these suggestions.

Analysis

Pets for People is best placed in Stage Three. It has established a solid foundation for a successful organization, having passed through the "vision to reality" stage. It is moving toward setting boundaries and parameters that will enable it to grow. The board has expanded beyond its original membership and moved from a circle of insiders, such as the executive director's sister, to outsiders who are asking critical questions of the organization. The founding executive director is still the central figure in the organization, which, as the organization has grown, has created difficult demands on his time. The need for more staff, better administrative systems, and increased client demand will undoubtedly stretch the organization's finances, forcing it to generate more income. The addition of staff will also challenge the organization to create more formal policies and procedures. On the program side, as the organization has become more visible the need for services has expanded—as evidenced by the long waiting list. Program expansion will in turn raise marketing, staffing, and financing issues, all characteristic of an organization in Stage Three.

Advice

There are several paths the organization can take to facilitate its journey through Stage Three and prepare it for Stage Four. Following are some of the choices it may make, depending on the board's and executive director's perceptions of the most pressing issues.

- Increase the number of staff. Unburdening the executive director by the use of volunteers or interns, or finding the resources to hire additional staff, is critical. The demands will only grow and one person will not be able to meet all of them. Without additional help the executive director will burn out and the organization will be poised to fail.

- Get technical assistance. The executive director needs some accounting expertise. Educating the executive director on basic accounting procedures and installing them in the organization is a must for the organization to maintain good standing with its constituents.

- Develop a budget and fundraising plan. A three-year budget for the organization should be developed. This will determine what financing needs to be in place.[10] Next, a fundraising plan can be created that specifies how the organization will meet its funding needs, including beginning to look at earned income sources.

- Develop a long-range plan for the organization. Since this will be the organization's first strategic plan, a brief one will probably suffice. This can be accomplished easily during a one-day retreat involving the board, staff, and key volunteers. They should focus on articulating the organization's history and values and examining its strengths, weaknesses, opportunities, and threats. The result should be a short document that outlines the key goals or areas of focus for the organization for the next two to five years. A strategic plan will guide key decisions that need to be made in each of the seven organizational arenas introduced in Chapter One: board, staff leadership, administrative systems, financing, staffing, products and services, and marketing.

- Train the board. Although the scenario does not indicate the board is troubled, the statement that the executive director is resisting their requests is a hint of impending conflict between the board and director. This conflict may be preempted or minimized by educating the board on its roles and responsibilities.[11]

---

[10] Stevens and Anderson (1997) provide sound advice on thinking through the finances of nonprofit organizations.

[11] For guidance on dealing with board conflicts or board-executive conflicts, see Angelica (1999; 2000).

Alms for Peace: *An Organization Embarking on Stage Four*

Alms for Peace was incorporated seven years ago. It began as the dream of the founder who wanted to create programs that would more broadly support world peace. The founder left her position at a reputable international organization because, although the organization could probably have supported her ideas, it did not offer the flexibility and autonomy she wanted. After one year of doing freelance consulting related to her ideas, she incorporated a 501(c)(3) and named herself executive director. She recruited board members who could advise her on different aspects of her program ideas. After seven months the newly formed agency hired a part-time staff person with expertise in both world peace concepts and business administration. In its third year the executive director negotiated with the board president, a personal friend, to step in as a full-time staff person for the agency.

Produce and Sustain

Over time, the friendship soured, and tension between the executive director and the staff friend began to build. Board members were pulled into the conflict and a period of high stress ensued. The conflict between the executive director and her friend was resolved by firing the friend. Because of the conflict a number of critical incidents occurred: some board members resigned, the board engaged in a strategic planning process, and a consultant was hired to assist the organization with board development. Three years later the conflict remains a painful and present memory—an experience neither the board nor the executive director wants to repeat.

Despite the stress, the organization has been very successful with its original programs. It has well-established administrative processes and procedures and handles its operational issues smoothly. Due to its program success and infrastructure stability, it has recently encountered many opportunities to expand its work. The executive director has pursued a variety of these ideas, adding staff and volunteers. Recently, the executive director has restructured the organization by dividing it into two distinct programs.

The executive director, still affected by the conflict, wants to ensure that the organization has a smooth and secure future. She is extremely excited about the opportunities to expand and to make a real impact on world peace. She loves the unique expertise the organization brings to the field and is proud of the fact that she has created something out of nothing. She believes her greatest challenges for the coming year include the following: to configure, staff up, and grow the two distinct areas of the organization; to maintain the clarity of the board-staff roles and relationships; and to create a comprehensive and well-packaged image of the organization.

Analysis

Alms for Peace is in the early phases of Stage Four. In contrast to Pets for People, Alms for Peace has already had significant changes in the board, a critical staff incident, significant program expansion, board training, and a strategic plan. In addition it has a well-functioning infrastructure. However, common to many early Stage Four organizations, the opportunity to grow and expand is staring the organization in the face. Increasing staff, restructuring to accommodate them, and wrestling with the board-staff role are also typical of organizations in early Stage Four. The need to package the organization—including image definition and creation of more promotional tools—is typical of the issues facing early Stage Four organizations. The heightened need to pay attention to both internal and external demands is often a dilemma of founding executive directors in early Stage Four organizations.

Advice

The executive director feels a need to expand some program areas, add staff, and figure out how staff should relate to each other. In addition, the executive wants to ensure that the board-staff relationship remains strong and sees a need for the organization to better define its public image. There are hints that the executive director is most enthused by the program development and may have less interest or skill in the internal management now needed. Several actions are indicated.

- Focus on marketing. Hire a marketing consultant to develop promotional tools for the organization. Word-of-mouth or rudimentary tools will no longer suffice. Clearly defining what the organization is and what it is not enables the organization to better attract clients and funders as well as lessen the confusion for board, staff, and volunteers. Additionally, clear and crisp promotional tools will enhance the public's image of the organization.[12]

- Refine the organizational chart. Clarify, or refine and record, the roles and relationships of staff. The organization will not be able to expand if staff roles and relationships are not reassessed, negotiated, and clearly delineated.

- Institutionalize annual board training. Educating the board members on their roles and responsibilities annually is now a priority. This allows long-term board members to raise questions while new members learn their roles.

- Develop an executive director performance review process. Early in Stage Four, the organization needs to address both internal structure and external image issues. This creates many demands on the executive director, whose role often changes. The annual performance review process clarifies where the executive director's focus should be and allows the executive director to do a self-

---

[12] For guidance on creating a marketing plan and marketing materials, see Stern (2001).

assessment and a professional development plan. It helps the board to stay on top of expectations and accountabilities as the organization changes and strengthens the board's role in focusing and monitoring the executive director's performance.

We Spell Relief: *An Organization in Stage Four*

We Spell Relief assists in disaster relief. The seventy-year-old organization, founded by influential members of a large city, employs ninety staff and has a broad base of secure funding. The diverse board represents the wide interests of the agency and focuses on policy and governance. The chief executive officer has primary responsibility for the administration and operations of the agency and only involves the board on policy issues, major future decisions, and fundraising. The organization has diversified its funding in the last twenty years. It has decreased its reliance on United Way funding from more than 50 percent to approximately 30 percent. In recent years the finance director position has been elevated to a vice president level position. Staffing has remained stable for the last few years and minimal growth is anticipated. Staff are hired, in part, on their ability to be team players. There are distinct levels of management with supervisor, manager, and director level positions.

Produce and Sustain

Programs have changed over the long history of the organization, but the organization is now faced with re-evaluating long-standing programs. Many employees are pushing the organization to consider riskier programs and to be more flexible in its personnel policies. The executive defines the following as strengths of the agency: the longevity and experience of the organization, management team, and staff (the executive has been in place for twenty-three years); the sharing of authority, responsibility, and trust among the board and staff; and the structural stability of the agency. Centralizing key functions, articulating the organization's culture and expectations for new staff, and reorganizing to make best use of key staff are issues the executive sees as pertinent to the organization's success.

Analysis

At seventy years old, with ninety employees, We Spell Relief is a well-established entity in Stage Four of its life. The leadership is stable and clear about roles and responsibilities, as is the board. The management of We Spell Relief is left to the executive while the board focuses on policy and strategic direction issues. The fact that funding is stable and diverse is also a clue that it is a Stage Four organization, since stable and diverse funding is needed to maintain and sustain organizations over many years. The hierarchical management structure noted here is often found in Stage Four organizations. The structure facilitates delegation and accountability in larger organizations. The stability of programs and even the need to seriously reevaluate a long-standing program is typical of mature organizations. Additionally, longevity and size of Stage Four organizations explain why centralization and orientation of new staff are critical issues. These appear to be issues for We Spell Relief as well. As is often the case in Stage Four organizations, there is a desire by the staff of this organization to be more flexible, more creative, and take more risks.

Advice

Since this organization is quite stable financially with little conflict at the leadership level, issues such as funding and board-staff relations are of less concern than running an effective and efficient organization. The organization appears to be highly efficient due to centralization of some key functions, articulation of the organization culture, and well-placed staff. If all is going well the organization would be wise to stay the course. However, many organizations in Stage Four hit a rut and need to find ways to be more flexible, more creative, take more risks, and deal with areas of rising tension. Even though things are going well now, We Spell Relief may want to consider the following to ensure continued success.

- Initiate an in-depth strategic planning process. Successful times offer an excellent opportunity for detailed introspection. A process to look broadly and deeply at the organization's strengths, weaknesses, opportunities, and threats may help avert crisis and position the agency well for the future.[13]

- Create an "innovation" department or process. Look for ways to support new ideas and new models. Organizations in Stage Four may lose the ability to innovate, take risks, and change.

- Assess the board's strengths and weaknesses. Chances are it has been operating the same way for quite some time. It may be due for some minor adjustments or even some major changes to perform most effectively.

- Get smart about marketing. The organization is well enough established to be strategic about what and how it promotes itself. Develop a comprehensive marketing plan to ensure the organization gets where it wants to go.[14]

---

[13] For guidance on creating a strategic plan, see Barry (1997).

[14] For guidance on creating a marketing plan and marketing materials, see Stern (2001).

Just Like Home: *An Organization in Stage Five*

Now in its sixth decade, Just Like Home Halfway House was one of the first shelters in the nation for homeless youth. The well-funded organization has a fairly broad funding base combining grants with federal and state funding. Until recently, many of the staff had been with the organization for more than fifteen years and all would have described the organization as an excellent place to work. The organization has had two prior executive directors, each having led the agency for about twenty-five years. The current executive director has been in the position five years, following in the footsteps of a highly autocratic predecessor. She is known throughout the community for her collaborative approach and impeccable integrity.

Review and Renew

As soon as she assumed the leadership of the organization, the new executive began to promote a more inviting organizational culture. Staff enthusiastically welcomed this positive shift. The executive director insisted on the agency becoming more culturally diverse to better meet the needs of the youth being served. She redirected the strengths of the organization from a wide, somewhat scattered geographic client base to a more focused one and has challenged the staff and board to serve those youth in highest need. The organization has been on a positive course for many years, but now faces some critical choices about the future of some of its key services. Meanwhile several important organization issues loom: many of the long-time staff are retiring or moving on to positions in other agencies, there are repercussions from a recent organization-wide restructuring, and an entirely new approach to services is under review by the board. The atmosphere in the organization is one of security in its existence, but it is shadowed by the anticipation of a major redefinition.

Analysis

Just Like Home is a Stage Five organization. The sense that the organization is on the verge of some dramatic shifts is a clue that the organization is moving beyond Stage Four. Its existence over several generations and its financial stability are testaments to its organizational maturity, as is its positive reputation with community and staff.

What distinguishes Just Like Home from a Stage Four organization is the number of critical changes it faces: the sentiment that there is a fresh, trustworthy new leader in place who is making important changes; the major geographic redirection of organization's service area; and the turnover of long-time staff. There is a general feeling of metamorphosis at Just Like Home. It is this kind of revitalizing, redirecting activity and atmosphere that characterize organizations in Stage Five.

Advice

Just Like Home is in a comfortable position. While there are major changes occurring, none of them are life threatening. This means that the leadership of the organization has the luxury of being more strategic about the changes. With the high staff turnover, especially among tenured employees, revitalizing the staff needs to be a key focus. The organization must also be patient. Employees need time to absorb staffing changes and restructuring. The board and key staff must also resolve the service delivery questions. This is a challenging yet exciting time for the organization. To navigate the challenges of Stage Five effectively the organization should consider the following:

- Engage in an in-depth strategic planning process.[15] There are several critical questions related to the programs and services of the organization. The board and key staff should do a careful assessment and thorough investigation of the options before implementing change.

- Review internal staff development systems. Staff turnover can be costly to the organization—both in real dollars and in morale. The organization should minimize the cost by maximizing its investment in the people who are currently employed in the organization.

- Ensure that internal systems are top-notch. With the number and magnitude of the changes occurring it would be easy to let internal systems slide. That would be like allowing the foundation of a house to crumble while putting on a new roof. It is important to maintain the foundation so that the organization can weather the changes successfully.

- Communicate frequently and openly. Staff changes and restructuring stress employees, and morale can take a nosedive. To improve morale, the executive director and board should communicate frequently with employees and key stakeholders about the changes. Communication can also include elements designed to build the staff's skills at managing change.

---

[15] For guidance on creating a strategic plan, see Barry (1997) or Allison and Kaye (1997).

Refugee Youth Center: *An Organization in Decline*

At eight years old, the Refugee Youth Center is struggling. The executive director came to the United States as a war refugee nearly ten years ago. He started the Refugee Youth Center to educate various refugee youth about their cultural heritage and to help preserve their cultures for future generations. The organization operates on a very limited budget. The executive director is part time and staff is hired when programs receive funding. The majority of programs are short term and since money is received only to operate programs, staff are laid off when programs end.

Decline and Dissolution

In the past few years a number of other agencies have begun serving refugee youth. Competition for funding is becoming even more acute. Additionally, the executive director has announced that he has some health problems. Rumors are circulating that the executive director has been behaving erratically. While untrue, the rumors have hurt the organization's reputation. Gradually, program funding, the executive director's attendance, and community interest in the agency is dwindling. Word of Refugee Youth Center's precarious position is spreading. Other agencies are unwilling to make referrals. The board of directors has contacted another youth service agency and refugee agency—both of which were founded by refugees with close ties to the Refugee Youth Center—to inquire about merging.

Analysis

Although eight years old and somewhere in Stage Three of its life, Refugee Youth Center is fast approaching demise. The precarious nature of the agency's funding and programming point to an organization on the verge of collapse. Add to this the absence of the executive director due to poor health, and it is easy to understand how the organization is on the brink of dissolution. The pervasive sense of "survival" is probably what motivated the board to actively engage in merger conversations with another agency.

Advice

There are several paths the organization can take to manage the complexities of a declining organization. Although difficult, probably the most honorable action the Refugee Youth Center can take is to close its doors. The board can engage in the following actions to put the organization to rest.[16]

- Hold a special board meeting. Ensure the board agrees about the state of the organization and the action steps that will be taken. Board ignorance or dissension can exacerbate the difficulties of the organization.

---

[16] Two publications may help nonprofits in decline: *Nonprofit Decline and Dissolution Project Report* (1987) and Angelica and Hyman (1997).

- Explore merger options. Develop a plan for determining whether or not merging with another agency is a viable option.[17] There are probably programs that are worth preserving—the board must decide how the programs can best be preserved. The board's decision to contact two other organizations with close ties is a good start.

- Meet with funders. Schedule face-to-face meetings with funders to explain what is happening and engage their support in helping the organization through this difficult stage. It is important to maintain good funder relations during this time of crisis.

- Develop a communications plan. It is apparent that rumors are circulating about the health of the organization. Additionally, the rumors about the executive director are unfair to him and not helpful for potential merger discussions. The board must decide how to address these rumors and keep them in check so that clients, staff, board, volunteers, and other friends of the organization are not harmed, and so that the many important accomplishments of the organization over its eight-year history are not forgotten.

---

[17] For guidance on deciding whether and how to merge, see La Piana (2000).

Chapter Four

Advice for Consultants Using the Model and Assessment Tool

CONSULTANTS WHO WORK WITH nonprofit organizations should find the life stages model and assessment tool in this book to be especially helpful. The usefulness for this model and tool for consultants can be enhanced when applied in tandem with the consulting model presented by Carol Lukas in her book *Consulting with Nonprofits: A Practitioner's Guide.*[18] Lukas outlines six stages of the consulting process.

Stage One: Contracting

Stage Two: Gathering and Analyzing Data

Stage Three: Planning the Work

Stage Four: Implementing and Monitoring

Stage Five: Sustaining Change and Evaluating Impact

Stage Six: Terminating the Consulting Project

The life stages model and assessment tool may be applied throughout the entire consulting process presented by Lukas, but especially at particular stages in the process. Following are some suggestions about how the model and tool can be used in several of those stages.

---

[18] Lukas (1998, 20).

Stage One: Contracting

This is the introduction stage, during which you determine the kind of help the organization needs, establish credibility, and formulate agreements with the client. Here, the assessment tool can help you determine where the organization has strengths and weaknesses and what its primary issues are. Sharing some of the life stages concepts with the client in the initial meeting can communicate credibility—that you really "know" nonprofit organizations.

Stage Two: Gathering and Analyzing Data

The purpose of this stage is to fully understand what the client needs in order to be successful and what actions will facilitate success. The assessment tool can be used as a diagnostic tool. Consultants can distribute the assessment tool to predetermined audiences. The data can then be analyzed to see where to focus the intervention.

Stage Three: Planning the Work

This stage is where you refine the organization's or group's goals, based on what you learned in the previous stage, and help the organization decide what strategies it will use to achieve those goals. Consultants can use the results of the assessment tool in the design of their intervention—to help focus and sequence it.

Stage Four: Implementing and Monitoring

In the fourth stage of the consulting process you and the client implement the plans that were created in Stage Three. You monitor the implementation over time to ensure that events or changes have the intended effect and goals are accomplished. You make adjustments as needed to keep the project successful. We have not found applications of the assessment tool at this stage.

Stage Five: Sustaining Change and Evaluating Impact

The purpose of this stage is for the client to assess the extent to which the plans or changes that have been implemented have accomplished the desired outcome. Consultants can readminister the assessment tool and compare pre- and post- responses to determine whether the intervention had the intended impact.

Stage Six: Terminating the Consulting Project

This stage involves formally ending the consulting relationship. It often includes a final debrief with the client. The consultant might broach the subject of organization life stages, using the model and assessment tool in this book as a way to discuss what stage the organization is currently in and to anticipate what other issues it might be poised to face.

In addition to these general applications of the life stages model and assessment tool to Lukas's consulting process, there are also certain consulting activities in which the model and tool can be applied. Following are some specific examples of this.

Strategic Planning

Concepts of the life stages model are helpful in many phases of a strategic planning process. Presentation of the concepts often helps people in organizations put their organizational history and future in context, assists in identifying organizational strengths, weaknesses, opportunities, and threats across the seven arenas, and offers ideas for possible critical issues facing the organization.

Executive Director Coaching

Discussing the various life stages of nonprofit development with their accompanying opportunities and obstacles offers perspective and reassurance to executive directors about the problems they are experiencing and the issues they are wrestling with. Having the executive director complete the assessment tool is also a useful aid in focusing coaching discussions.

Board Development

Presenting the life stages model to boards of directors or having them complete the assessment tool helps them place their organization on a continuum with other organizations. It often allays fears that their organization is in serious trouble because they see that the issues they are facing are typical of many nonprofits in their same stage. It will also help the board frame an agenda for their own development.

Collaboration Process Coaching

Introducing the life stages model to a multiorganizational collaborative offers insights into why tensions may exist within the collaborative. Many collaboratives are comprised of organizations in various life stages. These different levels of organizational maturity can create barriers for the collaborative. For example, a Stage Four member expects well-organized, timely reports, but a Stage Two member doesn't have any support staff, let alone the time to focus on these kind of administrative details. Having members complete the tool and then discuss the results early in the collaboration process can facilitate the success of the collaborative.

If nothing else, organization development consultants should familiarize themselves with the concepts of nonprofit organization life stages. The success of a consultant's work is in how well she or he assesses and assists organizations as they navigate through the various stages of development. Knowing what those stages are, how they are likely to be manifested, and the challenges and opportunities of moving through them is critical.

Afterword

JOHN W. GARDNER, American foundation executive, author, and public official, says, "Like people and plants, organizations have a life cycle. They have a green and supple youth, a time of flourishing strengths, and a gnarled old age...."[19] While not all organizations have a "gnarled old age," they do experience times in their life that feel gnarly. These are often times of transition and growth. Because transitions can be painful and frustrating, it's helpful to have a framework for understanding those transitions. Unlike people—and fortunately, like many plants—nonprofits have the capacity to regenerate, send out runners and new shoots, broad roots and branches, and even, as with some trees, generate new growth from their fallen trunks.

This book was written to provide a framework that would help nonprofits reach the wonderful place of continuous regeneration that we see in some established organizations. The nonprofit environment is a rich one, full of many choices and opportunities. Best wishes as your nonprofit grows and develops.

---

[19] Gardner, as quoted in Lippitt and Schmidt (1967).

Appendices

Appendix A

Bibliography

Allison, Michael, and Jude Kaye. *Strategic Planning for Nonprofit Organizations.* New York, NY: John Wiley and Sons, Inc. 1997.

Amherst H. Wilder Foundation. *Nonprofit Decline and Dissolution Project Report.* Saint Paul, MN: Fieldstone Alliance, 1987.

Angelica, Emil, and Vincent Hyman. *Coping with Cutbacks: The Nonprofit Guide to Success When Times Are Tight.* Saint Paul, MN: Fieldstone Alliance, 1997.

Angelica, Marion Peters. *Keeping the Peace: Resolving Conflict in the Boardroom.* Washington, DC: National Council for Nonprofit Boards, 2000.

Angelica, Marion Peters. *Resolving Conflict in Nonprofit Organizations.* Saint Paul, MN: Fieldstone Alliance, 1999.

Adams, Tom. "Executive Transitions: How Board and Executives Create Their Futures." *Nonprofit World* 126, no. 3 (1998) 48–52.

Adizes, Ichak. *Corporate Life Cycles: How and Why Corporations Grow and Die and What to Do About It.* Englewood Cliffs, NJ: Prentice-Hall, 1988.

Adizes, Ichak. "Organizational Passages: Diagnosing and Treating Life Cycle Problems of Organizations." *Organizational Dynamics* (Summer, 1979) 3–25.

Baxter, Harry. "Joining the Board of a Nonprofit Organization." Monograph. Saint Paul, MN: Management Assistance Project. (1987, 1988).

Bridges, William. *Managing Transitions: Making the Most of Change*. Reading, MA: Addison-Wesley Publishing Company, 1991.

Cameron, Kim S., Robert I. Sutton, and David A. Whetten.. *Readings in Organizational Decline: Frameworks, Research, and Prescriptions*. Cambridge, MA: Ballinger Publishing Company, 1988.

Carver, John, "The Founding Parent Syndrome: Governing in the CEO's Shadow." *Nonprofit World* 10, no. 5 (1992).

Chambliss, Arrington, Wayne Meisel, and Maura Wolf. *Light One Candle: Quotes for Hope and Action*. White Plains, NY: Peter Pauper Press, 1991.

Galbraith, Jay. "The Stages of Growth." *Journal of Business Strategy* 3, no. 4 (1982) 70–79.

Greiner, Larry E. "Evolution and Revolution as Organizations Grow." *Harvard Business Review* 50, no. 4 (1972) 37–46.

Haffron, F. *Organization Theory and Public Organizations: The Political Connection*. Englewood Cliffs, NJ: Prentice Hall, 1989.

Hambrick, Donald C., and Lynn M. Crozier. "Stumblers and Stars in the Management of Rapid Growth." *Journal of Business Venturing* 1 (1985) 31–45.

Hanks, Steven H., Collin J. Watson, Eric Jansen, and Gaylen N. Chandler. "Tightening the Life-Cycle Construct: A Taxonomic Study of Growth Stage Configurations in High-Technology Organizations." *Entrepreneurship Theory and Practice* 18, no. 2 (1993) 5–29.

Hummel, Joan M. *Starting and Running a Nonprofit Organization*. Minneapolis, MN: University of Minnesota Press, 1996.

Isabella, Lynn A. "The Effect of Career Stage on the Meaning of Key Organizational Events." *Journal of Organizational Behavior* 9, no. 4 (1988) 345–58.

Kazanjian, Robert K. "Relation of Dominant Problems to Stages of Growth in Technology-Based New Ventures." *Academy of Management Journal* 30, no. 2 (1988) 257–79.

Lippitt, Gordon L., and Warren H. Schmidt. "Crises in a Developing Organization." *Harvard Business Review* 45 (1967) 102–112.

La Piana, David. *The Nonprofit Mergers Workbook: The Leader's Guide to Considering, Negotiating, and Executing a Merger*. Saint Paul, MN: Fieldstone Alliance, 2000.

Lukas, Carol A. *Consulting with Nonprofits: A Practitioner's Guide*. Saint Paul, MN: Fieldstone Alliance, 1998.

Lundberg, C. "The Dynamic Organizational Contexts of Executive Succession: Considerations and Challenges." *Human Resource Management* 25, no. 2 (1986), 287–303.

Mancuso, Anthony. *How to Form a Nonprofit Corporation in All Fifty States.* 4th ed. Berkeley, CA: Nolo Press, 1997.

Mathiasen, Karl III. *Board Passages: Three Key Stages in a Nonprofit Board's Life Cycle.* Washington, DC: National Center for Nonprofit Boards, 1990.

Mattessich, Paul W., Marta Murray-Close, and Barbara R. Monsey. *Collaboration: What Makes it Work* 2nd ed. Saint Paul, MN: Fieldstone Alliance, 2001.

McNamara, Carter. "The Founder's Syndrome in Nonprofit Organizations." Unpublished paper. Saint Paul, MN: October 1998.

Miller, Lawrence M. *Barbarians to Bureaucrats: Corporate Life Cycle Strategies.* New York, NY: Ballantine Books, 1990.

Miller, Danny and Patrick H. Friesen. "A Longitudinal Study of the Corporate Life Cycle." *Management Science* 30, no. 10 (1984) 1161–83.

New York Nonprofits. "Organizational Life Cycles." 14 no. 5 (September-October 1997).

Piercy, James E., and Benjamin J. Forbes. "The Phases of the Chief Executive's Career." *Business Horizons* 34, no. 2 (1991), 20–22.

Scott, Mel R., and Richard Bruce. "Five Stages of Growth in Small Business." *Long Range Planning* 20, no. 3 (1987), 45–52.

Sharken Simon, Judith H. "A Model of Nonprofit Organization Lifecycles: A Journey to Oz." Master's Thesis, University of Minnesota College of Education and Human Development, 1998.

Smith, Ken G., Terence R. Mitchell, and Charles E. Summer. "Top-Level Management Priorities in Different Stages of the Organizational Life Cycle." *Academy of Management Journal* 28, no. 4 (1985) 799–820.

Stern, Gary J. *Marketing Workbook for Nonprofit Organizations.* Saint Paul, MN: Fieldstone Alliance, 1990; 2nd ed., 2001.

Stevens, Susan Kenny, and Lisa M. Anderson. *Life Cycles of Nonprofit Organizations.* Saint Paul, MN: The Stevens Group, Inc., 1993.

Winer, Michael, and Karen Ray. *Collaboration Handbook: Creating, Sustaining, and Enjoying the Journey.* Saint Paul, MN: Fieldstone Alliance, 1994.

Wolf, Thomas. *The Nonprofit Organization: An Operating Manual.* Englewood Cliffs, NJ: Prentice Hall, 1984.

Appendix B

Useful Resources

Organizations

The following organizations are helpful contacts about particular nonprofit organization concerns.

BoardSource
1828 L Street NW
Suite 900
Washington, DC 20036
(202) 452-6262 or (877) 892-6273
www.boardsource.org

BoardSource provides numerous publications as well as consulting and training to nonprofit boards of directors.

Fieldstone Alliance
60 Plato Boulevard East
Suite 150
Saint Paul, MN 55107
(800) 274-6024
www.FieldstoneAlliance.org
books@fieldstonealliance.org

Fieldstone Alliance publishes books in the fields of nonprofit management and community development. Its consulting, training, and research and demonstration projects provide solutions to issues facing nonprofits, funders, and the communities they serve.

The Foundation Center
79 Fifth Avenue, 8th Floor
New York, NY 10003-3076
(212) 620-4230
http://foundationcenter.org

This is a centralized location for information and connections to philanthropic resources. Offers courses, directories, libraries, and other resources on grant seeking.

Independent Sector
1200 18th Street NW
Suite 200
Washington, DC 20036
(202) 467-6100
www.independentsector.org

Independent Sector is a coalition of leading nonprofits, foundations, and corporations strengthening not-for-profit initiative, philanthropy, and citizen action. They offer resources and information to and about the nonprofit sector.

Jossey-Bass Publishers
989 Market Street
San Francisco, CA 94103
(877) 762-2974
www.josseybass.com

Jossey-Bass (an imprint of John Wiley & Sons) offers publications on various aspects of nonprofit management.

Management Assistance Program for Nonprofits (MAP)
2314 University Avenue W
Suite 28
Saint Paul, MN 55114
(651) 647-1216
http://mapnp.nonprofitoffice.com
info@mapfornonprofits.org

MAP has a wonderful web library with lots of free, downloadable resources for nonprofit organizations.

National Council of Nonprofit Associations
1011 Vermont Avenue NW
Suite 1002
Washington, DC 20036
(202) 962-0322
www.ncna.org

This is a network of state and regional associations of nonprofit organizations. It offers a link to those associations that will likely offer technical assistance, resources, and information for large and small nonprofit organizations.

Nonprofit Genie
www.genie.org

It's not an organization but a web site with information on a wide variety of nonprofit management concerns.

LarsonAllen Public Service Group
220 S Sixth Street, Suite 300
Minneapolis, MN 55402
(612) 397-3301
www.larsonallen.com

The LarsonAllen Public Service group provides a variety of consulting for nonprofits and has done considerable work on nonprofit life cycles.

TCC Group
Offices in Chicago, New York, and Philadelphia:

875 N Michigan Avenue, 31st Floor
Chicago, IL 60611
(312) 794-7780

50 East 42nd Street, 19th Floor
New York, NY 10017
(212) 949-0990

One Penn Center, Suite 410
Philadelphia, PA 19103
(215) 568-0399

www.tccgrp.com

The TCC Group has done some work and trainings in the area of nonprofit organization life cycles. They also offer assistance to nonprofit organizations through consulting and training.

Publications

The following resources may be helpful at various stages in the life of the organization. While there are many, many more, the ones listed below will at least head you in the right direction. To help you select publications to meet specific challenges, the publications are organized according to which arena have the most relevance.

Books[20]

Administrative systems

Galbraith, Jay R., and Edward E. Lawler III. *Organizing for the Future: The New Logic for Managing Complex Organizations.* San Francisco, CA: Jossey-Bass, 1993.

> *This book explores key issues of organizational design and identifies approaches for managing complex organizations in a changing global marketplace.*

Gills, John, and Jamie Whaley. *Nonprofit Personnel Polices.* Gaithersburg, MD: Aspen Publishers, 1998.

> *This is a loose-leaf manual offering sample personnel policies. It includes advice on how to steer clear of legal difficulties as well a way to get the forms on diskette.*

Hummel, Joan M. *Starting and Running a Nonprofit Organization.* Minneapolis, MN: University of Minnesota Press, 1996.

> *This is a basic primer on starting and running a nonprofit. It covers boards of directors, bylaws, gaining 501(c)(3) status, creating a mission, budgeting, and more.*

Mancuso, Anthony. *How to Form a Nonprofit Corporation in All Fifty States.* 4th ed. Berkeley, CA: Nolo Press, 1997.

> *This book, with compact disc of legal forms, provides step-by-step directions to gain legal nonprofit status.*

Financing

Angelica, Emil, and Vincent Hyman. *Coping with Cutbacks: The Nonprofit Guide to Success When Times Are Tight.* Saint Paul, MN: Fieldstone Alliance, 1997.

> *This explains the changing relationship between the nonprofit and government sectors and offers a new way to think about resource problems in a nonprofit. It includes worksheets and a six-step process for developing solutions to respond to shrinking resources.*

---

[20] Portions of this list were adapted from the annotated resources in Lukas (1998).

Kushner Ciconte, Barbara, and Jeanne Jacob. *Fund Raising Basics: A Complete Guide.* Gaithersburg, MD: Aspen Publishers, 1997.

> *This primer for newcomers to fundraising provides basic information on the field covering topics such as using direct mail, prospect research, and developing and evaluating a fundraising plan.*

McKinney, Jerome. *Effective Financial Management to Public and Nonprofit Agencies,* 2nd ed. Westport, CT: Praeger Publishers, 1995.

> *This assists managers in integrating financial management with other aspects of management. It introduces and explains several financial management strategies including zero-base budgeting and borrowing and debt management.*

McLaughlin, Thomas. *Streetsmart Financial Basics for Nonprofit Managers.* New York, NY: John Wiley & Sons, 1995.

> *A hands-on resource for nonprofit financial management, this book offers easy-to-understand explanations of critical aspects of financial management including budgeting, cash flow, internal controls, and audits.*

Rosso, Henry. *Achieving Excellence in Fundraising: A Comprehensive Guide to Principles, Strategies and Methods.* San Francisco, CA: Jossey-Bass, 1991.

> *This book covers the primary elements of the fundraising profession and offers expert guidance and examples from several fundraising professionals.*

Seltzer, Michael. *Securing Your Organization's Future: A Complete Guide to Fund-Raising Strategies.* New York, NY: The Foundation Center, 1987.

> *This describes strategies for acquiring long-term financial well being and explains fund-raising strategies.*

Steckel, Richard, Robin Simons, and Peter Lengsfelder. *Filthy Rich and Other Nonprofit Fantasies: Changing the Way Nonprofits Do Business in the 90's.* Berkeley, CA: Ten Speed Press, 1989.

> *This book describes how nonprofits can earn revenue and demonstrates operating a business venture in the charitable sector.*

Governance

Angelica, Marion Peters. *Keeping the Peace: Resolving Conflict in the Boardroom.* Saint Paul, MN: Fieldstone Alliance and Washington, DC: National Council for Nonprofit Boards, 2000.

> *This is a guide for dealing with the specific types of conflicts experienced by nonprofit boards of directors.*

Carver, John, and Miriam Mayhew Carver. *Reinventing Your Board: A Step-by-Step Guide to Implementing Policy Governance.* San Francisco, CA: Jossey-Bass, 1997.

This provides guidelines for implementing the Policy Governance Model and describes effective board decision making and crafting useful policies.

Carver, John. *Boards That Make a Difference: A New Design for Leadership in Nonprofit and Public Organizations.* San Francisco, CA: Jossey-Bass, 1990.

This book examines board governance, board literature, and board practices, analyzes common failures of board governance, and introduces the Policy Governance Model.

Duca, Diane J. *Nonprofit Boards: Roles, Responsibilities, and Performance.* New York, NY: John Wiley & Sons, 1996.

This reviews key aspects of nonprofit governance and answers questions and provides direction on areas such as board structure, board responsibilities, and effective board meetings.

Houle, Cyril. *Governing Boards: Their Nature and Nurture.* San Francisco, CA: Jossey-Bass, 1990.

This is a practical guide to issues and challenges of boards of public and nonprofit organizations.

A Public Trust in Private Hands: Understanding the Work of Nonprofit Boards. Washington, DC: National Center for Nonprofit Boards, 1994.

A thirteen-minute video highlighting the role and function of nonprofit board members, its message is conveyed through the eyes of board members who serve a variety of types of organizations.

O'Connell, Brian. *The Board Member's Book: Making a Difference in Voluntary Organizations.* New York, NY: The Foundation Center, 1993.

This book discusses finding, developing, and rewarding good board members and helps board members make the most of volunteering.

Pierson, Jane and Joshua Mint. *Assessment of the Chief Executive: A Tool for Governing Boards and Chief Executives of Nonprofit Organizations.* Washington, DC: National Center for Nonprofit Boards, 1995.

A tool for assessing the executive director, it covers the basic functions of the chief executive and is available in disk format.

Young, Dennis R., Robert M. Hollister, Virginia A. Hodgkinson, and Associates. *Governing, Leading, and Managing Nonprofit Organizations: New Insights from Research and Practice.* Washington, DC: Independent Sector, 1993.

This provides insights in meeting the challenges of governance and management and describes nonprofit management practices.

Marketing

Brinckerhoff, Peter C. *Mission-Based Marketing: How Your Not-for-Profit Can Succeed in a More Competitive World.* Dillon, CO: Alpine Guild, 1998.

> *A resource for building a market-driven organization that honors its mission and values, this book provides explanation and guidance on the marketing cycle, analyzing markets, and being mission-oriented.*

Lauer, Larry. *Communication Power: Energizing your Nonprofit Organization.* Gaithersburg, MD: Aspen Publishers, 1997.

> *A handbook that covers many aspects of internal and external communications, it provides information and how-to's on such areas as board communication, donor communication, and media relations.*

McLeish, Barry J. *Successful Marketing Strategies for Nonprofit Organizations.* New York, NY: John Wiley & Sons, 1995.

> *This book reviews basic marketing concepts and strategies, including many real-life examples. It covers internal and external analysis and how to implement strategic marketing.*

Rados, David L. *Marketing for Nonprofit Organizations.* 2nd. ed. Westport, CT: Auburn House, 1996.

> *This is a text that covers the field of marketing and discusses several arenas of marketing such as pricing, products, and advertising and offers advice on how to address them.*

Stern, Gary J. *Marketing Workbook for Nonprofit Organizations Vol. 1: Develop the Plan.* Saint Paul, MN: Fieldstone Alliance, 2nd ed. 2001.

> *This workbook explains nonprofit marketing and how to write a marketing plan. It includes worksheets to guide the process.*

Stern, Gary J. *Marketing Workbook for Nonprofit Organizations Vol. 2: Mobilize People for Marketing Success.* Saint Paul, MN: Fieldstone Alliance, 1997.

> *This describes how to mobilize an entire organization, its staff, volunteers, and supporters to accomplish a marketing goal using a one-to-one marketing plan. It includes worksheets to guide the process.*

Withers, Jean, and Carol Vipperman. *Marketing Your Service: A Planning Guide for Small Business.* North Vancouver, British Columbia: International Self-Counsel Press, 1987.

> *This guide explains basic marketing and provides thirty-two worksheets to assist in developing a specific marketing plan.*

Products and services

Allison, Michael, and Jude Kaye. *Strategic Planning for Nonprofit Organizations.* New York, NY: John Wiley & Sons, Inc. 1997.

This is a guide to writing a strategic plan. It includes a disk with worksheets.

Barry, Bryan W. *Strategic Planning Workbook for Nonprofit Organizations, Revised and Updated.* Saint Paul, MN: Fieldstone Alliance, 1997.

A guide to writing and implementing a strategic plan, it outlines five steps and provides worksheets to guide the planning process.

Bryson, John M. *Strategic Planning for Public and Nonprofit Organizations,* Revised Edition. San Francisco, CA: Jossey-Bass, 1995.

A comprehensive text on strategic planning. Introduces the Strategy Change Cycle planning process with detailed explanation of the cycle.

Bryson, John M. and Farnum K. Alston. *Creating and Implementing Your Strategic Plan: A Workbook for Public and Nonprofit Organizations.* San Francisco, CA: Jossey-Bass, 1997.

A companion workbook to John M. Bryson's Strategic Planning for Public and Nonprofit Organizations, *this provides detailed worksheets for all phases of the strategic planning process.*

Mattessich, Paul W., Marta Murray-Close, and Barbara R. Monsey. *Collaboration: What Makes it Work* 2nd ed. Saint Paul, MN: Fieldstone Alliance, 2001.

An in-depth analysis of the literature on collaborations, it extracts key factors that result in successful collaboration and suggests practical ways to apply those to collaborative projects.

Pappas, Alceste T. *Reengineering Your Nonprofit Organization: A Guide to Strategic Transformation.* New York, NY: John Wiley & Sons, 1995.

This offers a model for organizational change and redesign. It presents best practices, innovative strategies, and a rationale for the reengineering process.

Winer, Michael, and Karen Ray. *Collaboration Handbook: Creating, Sustaining, and Enjoying the Journey.* Saint Paul, MN: Fieldstone Alliance, 1994.

This describes a process for starting and operating a collaborative and includes worksheets to assist the process.

Wholey, Joseph, Harry P. Hatry, and Kathryn E. Newcomer. *Handbook of Practical Program Evaluation.* San Francisco, CA: Jossey-Bass, 1994.

A basic guide to program evaluation methods, it covers evaluation design, data collection procedures, and data analysis.

Staff leadership

Amherst H. Wilder Foundation. *Nonprofit Decline and Dissolution Project Report.* Saint Paul, MN: Fieldstone Alliance, 1987.

This publication helps an organization understand when it should consider dissolution and provides guidance on why, when, and how to go out of business gracefully.

Bridges, William. *Managing Transition.* Reading, MA: Addison-Wesley, 1991.

Managing Transition *describes the emotional impact of change on employees and what can be done to keep change from disrupting an entire organization. It provides practical techniques for bringing people on board with change.*

Brinckerhoff, Peter C. *Mission-Based Management: Leading Your Not-for-Profit into the Twenty-First Century.* Dillon, CO: Alpine Guild, 1994.

This publication identifies the necessary skills for successful nonprofit leadership and describes the ten biggest mistakes nonprofits make when planning for growth.

Bryson, John, and Barbara Crosby. *Leadership for the Common Good: Tackling Public Problems in a Shared-Power World.* San Francisco, CA: Jossey-Bass, 1992.

It includes practical information, negotiation techniques, and networking strategies useful for overcoming problems associated with multiple-agency projects.

Drucker, Peter F. *Managing the Nonprofit Organization.* New York, NY: HarperCollins, 1990.

This book describes the tasks, responsibilities, and practices involved in effective management of nonprofit organizations. The contents include analyzing the mission and performance of the organization, developing professional relationships, and practicing self-development.

Hodgkinson, Virginia A., and Richard W. Lyman. *The Future of the Nonprofit Sector.* Washington, DC: Independent Sector, 1989.

This explores how complex changes today affect the future of nonprofit organizations. It offers strategies for coping with economic, social, and political trends.

Knauft, E. B., Renee A. Berger, and Sandra T. Gray. *Profiles of Excellence: Achieving Success in the Nonprofit Sector.* Washington, DC: Independent Sector, 1991.

This book identifies four principles of outstanding nonprofit leadership: primacy of mission, effective leadership, maintaining a dynamic board, and strong development programs.

La Piana, David. *The Nonprofit Mergers Workbook: The Leader's Guide to Considering, Negotiating, and Executing a Merger.* Saint Paul, MN: Fieldstone Alliance, 2000.

This in-depth guide explains the advantages and disadvantages of merger, options for merging, and how to negotiate and complete the merger. Numerous worksheets and pointers keep the user on track to a successful conclusion.

Pfeiffer, Jeffrey. *Managing with Power: Politics and Influence in Organizations.* Boston, MA: Harvard Business School Press, 1992.

This details the role of power and influence in organizations and includes sections on sources of power, strategies for employing power, and power dynamics.

Salamon, Lester M. *Holding the Center: America's Nonprofit Sector at a Crossroads.* New York, NY: Nathan Cummings Foundation, 1997.

This book examines the changing role of nonprofits within fields such as health care, education, social services, and international aid. It provides charts and tables to illustrate spending, growth, and other trends within these fields.

Senge, Peter M. *The Fifth Discipline: The Art and Practice of the Learning Organization.* New York, NY: Doubleday, 1990.

This book describes five disciplines considered important in building a learning organization.

Wheatley, Margaret. *Leadership and the New Science: Learning about Organizations from an Orderly Universe.* San Francisco, CA: Barrett-Koehler, 1994.

This book summarizes new science discoveries and discusses the search for a simpler way to lead organizations and provides insights for organizing work, people, and life.

Staffing

Angelica, Marion Peters. *Resolving Conflict in Nonprofit Organizations.* Saint Paul, MN: Fieldstone Alliance, 1999.

A conflict resolution guide designed specifically for the unique characteristics of nonprofit organizations, it includes a process for resolving conflicts and guidance on choosing outside mediation.

Campbell, Katherine Noyes, and Susan J. Ellis. *The (Help!) I-Don't-Have-Enough-Time Guide to Volunteer Management.* Philadelphia, PA: Energize, Inc. 1995.

This book presents a step-by-step framework for creating a team approach to volunteer management, including the role of the volunteer manager, finding volunteers, and sharing the work of the volunteer program with everyone in the organization.

Henning, Joel P. *The Future of Staff Groups: Daring to Distribute Power and Capacity.* San Francisco, CA: Barrett-Koehler, 1997.

This includes information on building staff group capacity, defining staff group accountability and service, repositioning staff groups, and reinventing staff group roles.

Johnson, Sandra J., and Mary Ann Smith. *Valuing Differences in the Workplace: Theory-to-Practice Monograph Series.* Alexandria, VA: American Society for Training and Development, 1991.

This book describes concepts involving effectively managing diversity and valuing differences in the workplace. It assists in the process of shifting to a multicultural focus in the organization.

Kochman, Thomas. *Black and White Styles in Conflict.* Chicago, IL: University of Chicago Press, 1981.

This book analyzes differences in business styles, clarifies cultural reasons for communication differences, and provides a guide for crossing racial barriers.

Loden, Marilyn, and Judy B. Rosener. *Workforce America: Managing Employee Diversity as a Vital Resource.* Homewood, IL: Business One Irwin, 1991.

Workforce America *shows how to recognize organizational problems, foster teamwork, create comfortable working environments, develop leadership skills, and manage employee differences as assets.*

Lohmann, Roger A. *The Commons: New Perspectives on Nonprofit Organizations and Voluntary Action.* San Francisco, CA: Jossey-Bass, 1992.

This book describes the social, economic, and political structures and processes that characterize nonprofit organizations and encourage voluntary action.

Tannen, Deborah. *That's Not What I Meant! How Conversational Style Makes or Breaks Relationships.* New York, NY: Ballantine, 1986.

This book describes the nature of conversation and interpersonal communication and their impact on relationships.

Thomas, Roosevelt R. Jr. *Beyond Race and Gender: Unleashing the Power of Your Total Work Force by Managing Diversity.* New York, NY: AMACOM, 1991.

This book describes the process of creating and managing cultural diversity.

Periodicals

Chronicle of Philanthropy: The Newspaper of the Nonprofit World. Washington, DC: The Chronicle of Higher Education, Inc.

> *This is a biweekly newspaper covering issues related to managing nonprofit groups, technology, gifts and giving, grant makers, special interests of donors and board members, and fundraising.*

Foundation News. Washington, DC: Council on Foundations, Inc.

> *This bimonthly publication covers topics related to foundations and philanthropic trends.*

Nonprofit Management and Leadership Journal. San Francisco, CA: Jossey-Bass.

> *This quarterly journal offers readers the authoritative insights of top executives and scholars on the common concerns of nonprofit leaders in all settings.*

Nonprofit World: The National Nonprofit Leadership and Management Journal. Madison, WI: Society for Nonprofit Organizations.

> *This magazine includes in-depth articles on nonprofit management and leadership and sections on global thinking, fundraising, the boardroom, legal counsel, resources, nonprofit providers, people and technology, relevant reviews, and nonprofit briefs.*

Appendix C

Notes on the Development and Testing
of the Assessment Tool

TERRY DONOVAN, an independent consultant with expertise in developing assessment tools, developed the assessment tool. Terry began by reviewing the initial work on the nonprofit life cycle stages. He then developed a series of questions for each arena in all the stages. These questions were reviewed and revised and then sent out to twenty-plus executive directors representing agencies in each of the stages. This initial field test assessed whether the instrument accurately measured the organization's stage, as well as solicited general feedback about the instrument. The tool was tested again using more than forty readers during the initial field test of the manuscript. Each time, based on the responses, the instrument was revised. Consistency in question format, relevance of the questions within each stage, and progression and alignment of the questions across the stages were all modified. For the final edition, the questions were organized to better show the interaction between an organization's home stage and the various arenas, as this seemed to be the most useful format.

Since this is a relatively new tool, we would welcome information on how the tool is used, as well as comments and suggestions for improvement. Send your comments to Fieldstone Alliance, 60 Plato BLVD E, STE 150, Saint Paul, MN 55107, or e-mail them to books@fieldstonealliance.org.

Determine what life stage your organization is in

Buy copies of the assessment so your organization's leaders can give their input

You can buy and distribute individual copies of the assessment to a number of members of the organization, and the results can be collated and presented to interested parties such as the board of directors or key staff. You can tally your score manually or online at the publisher's web site at www.FieldstoneAlliance.org.

The authors designed this tool with these purposes in mind:

- To provide insights on the stages of development of nonprofit organizations.
- As a tool for executive directors, boards of directors, and consultants who want to help nonprofit organizations grow and develop.
- As a discussion tool between boards of directors and employees.
- To provide benchmarks against which nonprofit organizations can gauge themselves.

The assesment includes complete instructions for administering, scoring, and interpreting the results.

See ordering information for how to order.

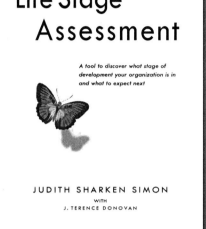

More results-oriented books from
FIELDSTONE ALLIANCE

The Nonprofit Mergers Workbook Part II
Unifying the Organization after a Merger
by La Piana Associates

Once the merger agreement is signed, the question becomes: How do we make this merger work? *Part II* helps you create a comprehensive plan to achieve *integration*—bringing together people, programs, processes, and systems from two (or more) organizations into a single, unified whole.

248 pages, includes CD-ROM   Item# 069415

Nonprofit Stewardship
A Better Way to Lead Your Mission-Based Organization
by Peter C. Brinckerhoff

You may lead a not-for-profit organization, but it's not *your* organization. It belongs to the community it serves. You are the steward—the manager of resources that belong to someone else. The stewardship model of leadership can help your organization improve its mission capability by forcing you to keep your organization's mission foremost. It helps you make decisions that are best for the people your organization serves. In other words, stewardship helps you do more good for more people.

272 pages, softcover   Item# 069423

Resolving Conflict in Nonprofit Organizations
The Leader's Guide to Finding Constructive Solutions
by Marion Peters Angelica

Helps you identify conflict, decide whether to intervene, uncover and deal with the true issues, and design and conduct a conflict resolution process. Includes exercises to learn and practice conflict resolution skills, guidance on handling unique conflicts such as harassment and discrimination, and when (and where) to seek outside help with litigation, arbitration, and mediation.

192 pages, softcover   Item# 069164

Strategic Planning Workbook for Nonprofit Organizations, Revised and Updated
by Bryan Barry

Chart a wise course for your nonprofit's future. This time-tested workbook gives you practical step-by-step guidance, real-life examples, one nonprofit's complete strategic plan, and easy-to-use worksheets.

144 pages, softcover   Item# 069075

Community Building

Community Building: What Makes It Work
by Wilder Research Center

Reveals twenty-eight keys to help you build community more effectively. Includes detailed descriptions of each factor, case examples of how they play out, and practical questions to assess your work.

112 pages, softcover   Item# 069121

Community Economic Development Handbook
by Mihailo Temali

A concrete, practical handbook to turning any neighborhood around. It explains how to start a community economic development organization, and then lays out the steps of four proven and powerful strategies for revitalizing inner-city neighborhoods.

288 pages, softcover   Item# 069369

The Community Leadership Handbook
by Jim Krile

Based on the best of Blandin Foundation's 20-year experience in developing community leaders—this book gives community members 14 tools to bring people together to make change.

240 pages, softcover   Item# 069547

The Fieldstone Alliance Nonprofit Guide to
Conducting Community Forums
by Carol Lukas and Linda Hoskins

Provides step-by-step instruction to plan and carry out exciting, successful community forums that will educate the public, build consensus, focus action, or influence policy.

128 pages, softcover   Item# 069318

The Creative Community Builder's Handbook
How to Transform Communities Using Local Assets, Art, and Culture
by Thomas Borrup

Creative community building is about bringing community development, arts and culture, planning and design, and citizen participation together to create sustainable communities. This book provides examples and tools to help community builders utilize human cultures and the creativity in everyone.

272 pages, softcover   Item# 069474

Collaboration

Collaboration Handbook
Creating, Sustaining, and Enjoying the Journey
by Michael Winer and Karen Ray

Shows you how to get a collaboration going, set goals, determine everyone's roles, create an action plan, and evaluate the results. Includes a case study of one collaboration from start to finish, helpful tips on how to avoid pitfalls, and worksheets to keep everyone on track.

192 pages, softcover   Item# 069032

For current prices, a catalog, or to order call 800-274-6024

Collaboration: What Makes It Work, 2nd Ed.

*by Paul Mattessich, PhD, Marta Murray-Close, BA,
and Barbara Monsey, MPH*

An in-depth review of current collaboration research. Major findings are summarized, critical conclusions are drawn, and twenty key factors influencing successful collaborations are identified. Includes The Wilder Collaboration Factors Inventory, which groups can use to assess their collaboration.

104 pages, softcover   Item# 069326

A Fieldstone Alliance Nonprofit Guide to
Forming Alliances

by Linda Hoskins and Emil Angelica

Helps you understand the wide range of ways that they can work with others—focusing on alliances that work at a lower level of intensity. It shows how to plan and start an alliance that fits a nonprofit's circumstances and needs.

112 pages, softcover   Item# 069466

The Nimble Collaboration
Fine-Tuning Your Collaboration for Lasting Success

by Karen Ray

Shows you ways to make your existing collaboration more responsive, flexible, and productive. Provides three key strategies to help your collaboration respond quickly to changing environments and participants.

136 pages, softcover   Item# 069288

Lobbying & Advocacy

The Lobbying and Advocacy Handbook for Nonprofit Organizations
Shaping Public Policy at the State and Local Level

by Marcia Avner

The Lobbying and Advocacy Handbook is a planning guide and resource for nonprofit organizations that want to influence issues that matter to them. This book will help you decide whether to lobby and then put plans in place to make it work.

240 pages, softcover   Item# 069261

The Nonprofit Board Member's Guide to Lobbying and Advocacy

by Marcia Avner

Written specifically for board members, this guide helps organizations increase their impact on policy decisions. It reveals how board members can be involved in planning for and implementing successful lobbying efforts.

96 pages, softcover   Item# 069393

Power in Policy
A Funder's Guide to Advocacy and Civic Participation

edited by David F. Arons

Increasingly, foundations are finding that participation in public decision making is often a critical component in reaching the impact demanded by mission-related goals. For those weighing precisely what role foundations should play, the mix of real-life examples, practical advice, and inspiration in this book are invaluable.

320 pages, softcover   Item# 069458

Finance

Bookkeeping Basics
What Every Nonprofit Bookkeeper Needs to Know

by Debra L. Ruegg and Lisa M. Venkatrathnam

Complete with step-by-step instructions, a glossary of accounting terms, detailed examples, and handy reproducible forms, this book will enable you to successfully meet the basic bookkeeping requirements of your nonprofit organization.

128 pages, softcover   Item# 069296

Coping with Cutbacks
The Nonprofit Guide to Success When Times Are Tight

by Emil Angelica and Vincent Hyman

Shows you practical ways to involve business, government, and other nonprofits to solve problems together. Also includes 185 cutback strategies you can put to use right away.

128 pages, softcover   Item# 069091

Financial Leadership for Nonprofit Executives
Guiding Your Organization to Long-term Success

by Jeanne Peters and Elizabeth Schaffer

Provides executives with a practical guide to protecting and growing the assets of their organizations and with accomplishing as much mission as possible with those resources.

144 pages, softcover   Item# 06944X

Venture Forth! The Essential Guide to Starting a Moneymaking Business in Your Nonprofit Organization

by Rolfe Larson

The most complete guide on nonprofit business development. Building on the experience of dozens of organizations, this handbook gives you a time-tested approach for finding, testing, and launching a successful nonprofit business venture.

272 pages, softcover   Item# 069245

For current prices or to order visit us online at www.FieldstoneAlliance.org

Marketing

The Fieldstone Alliance Nonprofit Guide to Conducting Successful Focus Groups
by Judith Sharken Simon

Shows how to collect valuable information without a lot of money or special expertise. Using this proven technique, you'll get essential opinions and feedback to help you check out your assumptions, do better strategic planning, improve services or products, and more.

80 pages, softcover   Item# 069199

Marketing Workbook for Nonprofit Organizations Volume I: Develop the Plan
by Gary J. Stern

Don't just wish for results—get them! Here's how to create a straightforward, usable marketing plan. Includes the six Ps of Marketing, how to use them effectively, a sample marketing plan, tips on using the Internet, and worksheets.

208 pages, softcover   Item# 069253

Marketing Workbook for Nonprofit Organizations Volume II: Mobilize People for Marketing Success
by Gary J. Stern

Put together a successful promotional campaign based on the most persuasive tool of all: personal contact. Learn how to mobilize your entire organization, its staff, volunteers, and supporters in a focused, one-to-one marketing campaign. Comes with *Pocket Guide for Marketing Representatives*. In it, your marketing representatives can record key campaign messages and find motivational reminders.

192 pages, softcover   Item# 069105

Board Tools

The Best of the Board Café
Hands-on Solutions for Nonprofit Boards
by Jan Masaoka, CompassPoint Nonprofit Services

Gathers the most requested articles from the e-newsletter, *Board Café*. You'll find a lively menu of ideas, information, opinions, news, and resources to help board members give and get the most out of their board service.

232 pages, softcover   Item# 069407

The Nonprofit Board Member's Guide to Lobbying and Advocacy
by Marcia Avner

Written specifically for board members, this guide helps organizations increase their impact on policy decisions. It reveals how board members can be involved in planning for and implementing successful lobbying efforts.

96 pages, softcover   Item# 069393

Keeping the Peace
by Marion Angelica

Written especially for board members and chief executives, this book is a step-by-step guide to ensure that everyone is treated fairly and a feasible solution is reached.

48 pages, softcover   Item# 860127

Funder's Guides

Community Visions, Community Solutions
Grantmaking for Comprehensive Impact
by Joseph A. Connor and Stephanie Kadel-Taras

Helps foundations, community funds, government agencies, and other grantmakers uncover a community's highest aspiration for itself, and support and sustain strategic efforts to get to workable solutions.

128 pages, softcover   Item# 06930X

A Funder's Guide to Evaluation: Leveraging Evaluation to Improve Nonprofit Effectiveness
by Peter York

More and more funders and nonprofit leaders are shifting away from proving something to someone else, and toward *im*-proving what they do so they can achieve their mission and share how they succeeded with others. This book includes strategies and tools to help grantmakers support and use evaluation as a nonprofit organizational capacity-building tool.

160 pages, softcover   Item# 069482

A Funder's Guide to Organizational Assessment
Tools, Processes, and Their Use in Building Capacity
by GEO

In this book, funders, grantees, and consultants will understand how organizational assessment can be used to build the capacity of nonprofits, enhance grantmaking, impact organizational systems, and measure foundation effectiveness.

216 pages, CD-ROM included   Item# 069539

Power in Policy
A Funder's Guide to Advocacy and Civic Participation
edited by David F. Arons

Increasingly, foundations are finding that participation in public decision making is often a critical component in reaching the impact demanded by mission-related goals. For those weighing precisely what role foundations should play, the mix of real-life examples, practical advice, and inspiration in this book are invaluable.

320 pages, softcover   Item# 069458

For current prices, a catalog, or to order call 800-274-6024

Strengthening Nonprofit Performance
A Funder's Guide to Capacity Building
by Paul Connolly and Carol Lukas
This practical guide synthesizes the most recent capacity-building practice and research into a collection of strategies, steps, and examples that you can use to get started on or improve funding to strengthen nonprofit organizations.

176 pages, softcover   Item# 069377

Violence Prevention & Intervention

The Little Book of Peace
24 pages (minimum order 10 copies)   Item# 069083
*Also available in **Spanish** and **Hmong**.*

Journey Beyond Abuse: A Step-by-Step Guide to Facilitating Women's Domestic Abuse Groups
208 pages, softcover   Item# 069148

Moving Beyond Abuse: Stories and Questions for Women Who Have Lived with Abuse
(Companion guided journal to *Journey Beyond Abuse*)
88 pages, softcover   Item# 069156

Foundations for Violence-Free Living:
A Step-by-Step Guide to Facilitating Men's Domestic Abuse Groups
240 pages, softcover   Item# 069059

On the Level
(Participant's workbook to *Foundations for Violence-Free Living*)
160 pages, softcover   Item# 069067

What Works in Preventing Rural Violence
94 pages, softcover   Item# 069040

ORDERING INFORMATION

Order online, or by phone or fax

Online: www.FieldstoneAlliance.org
E-mail: books@fieldstonealliance.org

Call toll-free: 800-274-6024
Internationally: 651-556-4509

Fax: 651-556-4517

Mail: Fieldstone Alliance
Publishing Center
60 Plato BLVD E, STE 150
St. Paul, MN 55107

Our NO-RISK guarantee

If you aren't completely satisfied with any book for any reason, simply send it back within 30 days for a full refund.

Pricing and discounts

For current prices and discounts, please visit our web site at www.FieldstoneAlliance.org or call toll free at 800-274-6024.

Quality assurance

We strive to make sure that all the books we publish are helpful and easy to use. Our major workbooks are tested and critiqued by experts before being published. Their comments help shape the final book and—we trust—make it more useful to you.

Visit us online

You'll find information about Fieldstone Alliance and more details on our books, such as table of contents, pricing, discounts, endorsements, and more, at www.FieldstoneAlliance.org.

Do you have a book idea?

Fieldstone Alliance seeks manuscripts and proposals for books in the fields of nonprofit management and community development. To get a copy of our manuscript submission guidelines, please call us at 800-274-6024. You can also view them on our web site at www.FieldstoneAlliance.org.

CPSIA information can be obtained at www.ICGtesting.com
Printed in the USA
BVOW05s0509230713

326699BV00010B/338/P